BEJEWELED

Penny Proddow

BEJEWELED

GREAT DESIGNERS
CELEBRITY STYLE

Harry N. Abrams, Inc., Publishers

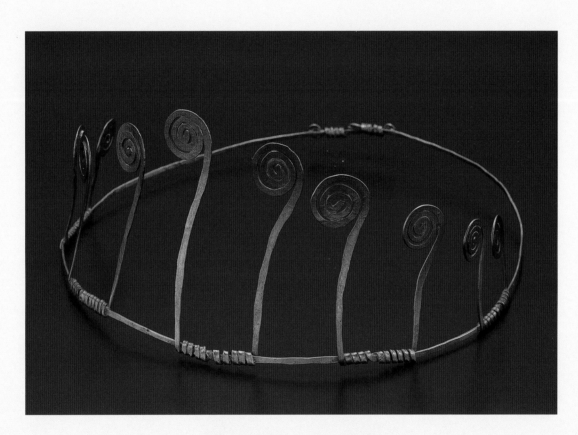

Marion Fasel

Contents

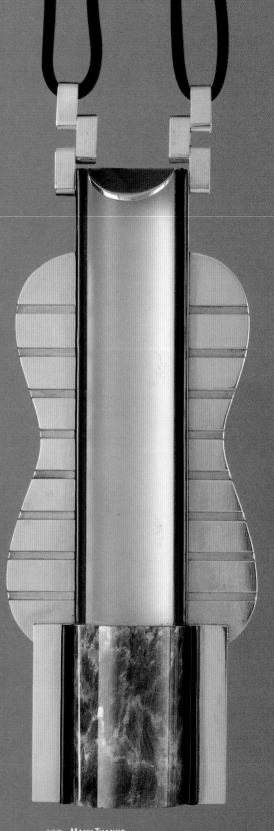

FOR RALPH

EDITOR: ELLEN NIDY

DESIGNER: CAROL ROBSON

JACKET DESIGN: GARRETT YANKOU

Library of Congress Cataloguing-in-Publication Data

Proddow, Penny.

    Bejeweled : great designers, celebrity style / by Penny Proddow and Marion Fasel.
        p. cm.
    Includes bibliographical references.
    ISBN 0–8109–0616–3
    1. Jewelry—History—20th century. 2. Jewelers—Biography. I. Fasel, Marion. II. Title.

NK7310 .P76 2001
739.27'09'04–dc21   2001022854

Printed and bound in Hong Kong
10 9 8 7 6 5 4 3 2 1

Harry N. Abrams, Inc.
100 Fifth Avenue
New York, N.Y. 10011
www.abramsbooks.com

Endpaper: Elsa Peretti transformed the scarf, a seventies staple, into a glamorous golden mesh necklace.

Page 2: A gold temple brooch made by Bulgari around 1972 with rock crystal columns and diamond accents points to the firm's Greek heritage.

Page 3: The Narcisse gold dog collar plaque by Lalique features two enamel figures surrounded by blue and green enamel chrysanthemums.

Page 5: A cabochon ruby heart brooch by Verdura wrapped in a diamond ribbon.

Page 6: The sapphires in Daisy Fellowes's diamond and gold pigeon-wing brooch by Boivin were specially cut to look like feathers.

Page 7: English art historian Sir Kenneth Clark bought his wife one of the few tiaras Calder ever made from the Freddy Mayor Gallery in England. The delicate brass jewel, a little circlet with a row of eight tapered spiral finials, undoubtedly turned a few crowned heads on formal occasions.

Page 8: A pavé-set Montana sapphire and silver butterfly brooch made by JAR around 1987 has white diamonds in platinum on the wings, and rose diamonds in silver on the body. A 3.89 antique cushion-cut diamond shines at the center of the insect.

Page 10, left: The Winter Landscape pendant, designed by Lalique around 1900, has an enamel scene of freshly fallen snow in the forest, framed in gold boughs with marquise-cut blue glass pine cones and a pear-shape gray pearl. Page 10, right: A pendant designed by Lalique around 1905 has two plique-à-jour enamel cobras framing a blue-green glass cameo of a woman draped in transparent fabric.

Table of contents page: A piece of frosted crystal is at the center of Gérard Sandoz's labradorite, lacquer, pink and white gold Guitar pendant. The jewel is suspended from a black silk cord necklace.

INTRODUCTION

Jewelry at its best is much more than just an accessory. The style and design of a jewel can illuminate a moment in time and reveal things about a culture. Details about life in ancient Greece—prosperity, a passion for myths, and advanced technical expertise—shine through in the gold jewelry from the fourth century B.C. In the seventeenth century, cameos chronicled famous nobles and popular literary figures; their faces were literally carved in gemstones. The extravagance of the seventeenth-century French court at Versailles is mirrored in Louis XIV's extraordinary collection of big diamonds.

In the twentieth century the sheer number of jewelry styles point to the constant changes in the economy, lifestyle, technology, fashion, and art. There were moments of avant-garde artistry and periods when accessible styles gained great popularity with large audiences, as well as plenty of looks that fell somewhere in between these two extremes. These huge trend swings mean that a lot of different jewelers came and went. The ones who stood out were image makers and pioneers, talents who were adept at translating the cultural shifts into magnificent designs.

This book has a sampling of many of the great twentieth century jewelry styles. There are masterpieces large and small, made with precious or semiprecious stones. Most pieces are rendered in platinum or gold, but there are those done in silver and brass too. What unites the jewelry is the quality of modernity as it was constantly redefined over the century. Each jewel was made by a designer who was absolutely in sync with their times.

A dog collar plaque made by Lalique around 1900 shows two blue enamel revelers playing their pipes among black enamel and diamond cherry blossom trees.

THE BIG NAMES

In the past the success of a precious jeweler hinged on one thing: a royal appointment. There was simply no better endorsement. To be the king's jeweler was a guarantee that other members of the court would patronize your establishment. Every royal had their favorite. For Napoleon it was Nitot, a jeweler known for grand trappings that matched the imperial style of the First Empire in France. During the mid-nineteenth century the fashionable Empress Eugénie of France liked the feminine diamond designs with bows, swags, and flowers from Bapst. The British royal family has been faithful to Garrard since 1843. Conservative designs centering on huge diamonds endeared the British firm to the royal family.

On a 1961 state visit to Paris, the President and Mrs. Kennedy attended a gala reception at Versailles. The First Lady pinned diamond brooches by Van Cleef & Arpels in her bouffant hairdo, creating the illusion of a modern tiara.

Things changed for jewelers in the twentieth century. The most high profile people were not royals but celebrities. American heiresses and socialites, queens of the gossip columns and glossy magazines counted among a jeweler's essential clients. The patronage of Barbara Hutton, Daisy Fellowes, Jackie Kennedy, Marjorie Merriweather Post, or the Duchess of Windsor was the equivalent of a royal appointment. These women were style icons. Their purchases inspired others to shop in the same places.

Hollywood also played a key role in the fortunes of jewelers in the twentieth century. Jewelers collaborating with production crews, loaning jewels as well as store space for location shoots, became part of the movies, the most glamorous medium of the century. Tiffany's role in *Breakfast at Tiffany's* stands out as the best example of how movies can sprinkle a jeweler with stardust and create a lasting celebrity image. Off-screen, movie stars like Gloria Swanson, Merle Oberon, and Elizabeth Taylor brought movie star magic to the jewels they wore and attention to the jewelers who made them. Just like the opening of Parliament, where the British royal family arrives decked out in treasures, the annual parade of movie stars down the red carpet at the Academy Awards ceremony is a show of jewelry at its brightest. The display is covered by the media worldwide and the jewelry is reviewed down to the last carat.

In this century of celebrity, five jewelers—Tiffany, Cartier, Van Cleef & Arpels, Harry Winston, and Bulgari—have risen to the top as world-class stars, the big names. This group has been nicknamed the Fifth Avenue jewelers, because they all have a store on Fifth Avenue in New York City. A strong presence in the media capital of the world contributes to international recognition. (Several magnificent jewelers that don't have a store in New York remain regional treasures.) But Fifth Avenue isn't all these jewelers have in common.

Big gem transactions are one aspect of being a jeweler to a king or a Hollywood queen. All the Fifth Avenue jewelers have sold storied, dazzling, and expensive gems. Bulgari acquired the Pasha of Egypt, a 41.06-carat octagonal diamond, for Barbara Hutton in the fifties. Cartier made headlines in 1969 when it sold Richard Burton the 69.42-carat pear-shape diamond, a gift for his wife Elizabeth Taylor. The gem, named the Taylor-Burton Diamond, cost just over a million dollars, a record-breaking price at the time. One of the biggest gem transactions at Tiffany was a purchase the jeweler made for itself. The 128.51-carat golden color

Audrey Hepburn gazes in the Tiffany windows in *Breakfast at Tiffany's* (1959). The popularity of the star and the movie made the firm's flagship New York store a tourist attraction.

Tiffany diamond, bought in 1879, has become an emblem of the firm. Claude Arpels of Van Cleef & Arpels brought the 114.30-carat Blue Princess sapphire from India in the 1950s for American socialite Florence Gould. Harry Winston sold more big diamonds than the other four jewelers. The Duchess of Windsor discovered her 31.36-carat McLean Diamond at Harry Winston. And Marjorie Merriweather Post purchased the 30.82-carat deep blue heart-shape diamond, called the Blue Heart, from Winston in 1964.

Major gem transactions are key for a jeweler, but in reality they are no more than a prerequisite to becoming a major jeweler. What separates a jeweler from a gem dealer, what makes a twentieth-century jeweler the equivalent of a royal favorite, is irresistible jewelry. Each one of the Fifth Avenue jewelers had a golden era of design when the firm's identity was established. The time frame coincided with visionary leadership at each one. Bulgari came of age in the late sixties with jewels that paired sleek modern elements with motifs from the classical world. Cartier emerged in 1925 as a jeweler with a passion for exotic animals and faraway lands like India, Egypt, and China. In the case of Bulgari and Cartier, the firms' individual looks didn't fully come together until the third generation. At both firms, a set of three young brothers took charge and energized the operations. Charles Lewis Tiffany, the founder of Tiffany, organized the idea of an emporium and started the something for everyone approach in the 1900s. Van Cleef & Arpels began its clever updates of traditional French court designs, like bows and flowers, in the twenties. It was a family affair at the firm. Numerous members and two generations of the Van Cleef and Arpels families guided the company during its creative peak. At Harry Winston, it was the man himself who made the firm's reputation for formal diamond jewelry in the 1950s.

Tiffany, Cartier, Van Cleef & Arpels, Harry Winston, and Bulgari all rose to prominence in the twentieth century. Four of the five have been honored with museum exhibitions. Some of them have been the subject of more than one major show. All five have inspired monographs chronicling their achievements.

Elizabeth Taylor glowed at a 1970 party in the 69.42-carat pear-shape diamond Richard Burton bought from Cartier. Around the time this photo was taken, the jewel was dubbed the Taylor-Burton Diamond after the world-famous couple.

Mrs. George Gould's triple strand of natural pearls by Tiffany cost her railroad magnate husband about a million dollars at the turn of the century.

TIFFANY

Audrey Hepburn turned Tiffany into a Hollywood star in the 1959 movie *Breakfast at Tiffany's.* Her character Holly Golightly, who was the epitome of New York glamour and urban sophistication, raved about the jeweler. "Nothing bad could ever happen to you at Tiffany's," she often said. She liked to walk around outside in the morning eating a Danish, sipping coffee, and looking at the jewelry in the windows. She liked to talk to the salesmen inside. Tiffany lifted her spirits when she had the "mean reds," a case of depression worse than the blues. It was a quiet place where there were big diamonds to dream about and a few things to buy for under ten dollars such as a sterling silver telephone dialer or the price of engraving a ring from a Cracker Jack box.

The character of Tiffany, as it was portrayed in the movie, had been scripted years before by its eponymous founder, Charles Lewis Tiffany. Since the start-up of the firm in 1837, his ambition was to have range in the inventory. Both high end and low end were dear to Mr. Tiffany. In 1858 he made 50-cent souvenir pendants from the surplus cable of the first trans atlantic phone lines. Three years later, Tiffany created a set of seed pearl jewels for Mary Todd Lincoln to wear at her husband's presidential inauguration. The unifying aspect of all the merchandise was good quality. Even the cable in Tiffany's souvenir pendants was carefully mounted in a brass ferrule so the wire wouldn't fray.

A Tiffany necklace shows all the elements popular in diamond and platinum jewelry around 1900: a garland choker, garland swags, and fancy pendants with large round diamonds.

A dog collar made by Tiffany in 1904 features gold Renaissance-style grillwork, pastel pink and green enamel, as well as turquoise, pearl, and diamond accents.

An iris brooch made by Tiffany designer Paulding Farnham for his wife, sculptor Sally James Farnham, around 1900. The flower has a pink-red rhodolite and diamond blossom, and a green demantoid garnet stem.

The press called Charles Lewis Tiffany "the King of Diamonds," because of the impressive number of gems he packed into his store.

A Tiffany diamond was every bit the equal of its European counterparts at the turn of the century. The firm imported crown jewels and large gems from overseas. In 1887 buyers scooped up more than half of the French crown jewels sold at auction for American clients, including Mrs. Joseph Pulitzer and Mrs. Bradley Martin. On home soil, Tiffany did great takes on the regal platinum and diamond jewelry styles of the era.

Daytime jewels in the inventory showed Tiffany knew quite a bit about what was happening at all echelons of European jewelry. The American jeweler appreciated Far Eastern art as much as the Art Nouveau crowd in Paris. It used Japanese motifs in jewelry as well as silver pitchers, vases, and trays. Tiffany also followed the European trend for revivalist jewelry but often split with its overseas counterparts in the execution of details. Many European jewelers took pains to replicate the art of previous ages down to the last gem. Tiffany frequently improvised on color schemes, matching the enamels of its Renaissance- and Rococo-style jewels to the colors in vogue. The trend for color-coordinated jewelry and clothes was dubbed "jewelry costuming" by The Jewelers Circular in 1907.

Some of the firm's finest jewels did not reference foreign work at all. Tiffany had its own bright ideas. One of them was big flower brooches. These showpieces flourished at international competitions, holding their own against designs from the world's greatest jewelers. The premise behind the flower brooches was simple; designer Paulding Farnham made them as lifelike as a jeweler could. The jewels were almost as big as real flowers. One Lawson Pink carnation was life-size and a bearded iris reached a length of 9½ inches. Farnham recreated the flowers' actual colors with a broad spectrum of semiprecious stones. He used pink tourmalines on carnations, purple-blue Montana sapphires, and pink-red rhodolite for irises. Grass-green demantoid garnets filled in leaves and stems.

Charles Lewis Tiffany's idea of quality inventory at every level has been maintained throughout the twentieth century. To stay in step with fashion, the firm updates collections seasonally. And over the years it has hired European byline designers including Jean Schlumberger, Elsa Peretti, and Paloma Picasso to create fashion-forward jewelry. Tiffany's achievements in the jeweled arts have been recognized with a museum exhibition and several books. The most comprehensive, *Tiffany's 20th Century* by Design Director John Loring, features a photo of Audrey Hepburn from *Breakfast at Tiffany's* on the cover. The movie still was the perfect image for the jewelry book. Hepburn's portrayal of Holly Golightly has become as much a symbol of the firm as its famous blue box.

ESTABLISHED: 1837
FOUNDER: Charles Lewis Tiffany (1812–1902)
SELECT BOOKS: Loring, John. *Tiffany Jewels*. New York: Harry N. Abrams, 1999; Purtell, Joseph. *The Tiffany Touch*. New York: Random House, Inc., 1971.
EXHIBITION: 1987, Chicago. *Tiffany: 150 Years of Gems and Jewelry*. The Field Museum of Natural History.
SOME MOVIE CREDITS: *Breakfast at Tiffany's* (1959), *Sleepless in Seattle* (1993), *The Muse* (1999).
LOCATIONS: Tiffany has over 100 stores in 16 countries. The flagship is in New York.

CARTIER

Silver screen star Merle Oberon, who in the thirties was just as famous for her jewelry as her beauty, gave one Hollywood reporter a behind-the-scenes look at the comings and goings of celebrities at Cartier when he asked her if her unusual emerald bead necklace was by the avant-garde couturier Elsa Schiaparelli. "No, but she almost got it!" replied Oberon. "I saw it at Cartier in Paris, and I went back a second time to look at it. The salesman said someone else was interested, but I only half believed him. The next time I went in, the necklace was not in the case. My mysterious rival had been looking at it in one of the little private rooms. Still I hesitated because the design was so exotic—so unlike the classic setting for precious stones. The next day I walked right by the shop, not intending to be tempted again, but Mme. Schiaparelli was just coming out. Instantly I knew why she had been there, and assumed she had the necklace right in her handbag. I must have looked my disappointment when I got back to the hotel, because Mr. Korda, in his direct way, put on his hat and went out. He walked across to the shop; the necklace was still there and he bought it."

The Cartier brothers, Pierre (1878–1965), Louis (1875–1942), and Jacques (1884–1942), made the firm a destination for celebrities in London, Paris, and New York between the two world wars. Jacques lived in London and managed the firm's branch on New Bond Street. Pierre directed the Fifth Avenue branch in New York. And both men traveled on Marco Polo-like expeditions to distant places, including Russia and India, to buy gems and serve clients. At the rue de la Paix Paris flagship, Louis and his design staff, including creative director Jeanne Toussaint (1887–1978), masterminded the firm's exotic precious jewelry.

In the midst of an Egyptian fashion frenzy ignited by Howard Carter's discovery of Tutankamen's tomb in 1922, Cartier made a number of boxes and jewels incorporating antiquities such as calcite plaques and little faience statuettes. Ancient Egyptian scarabs embellished with modern gemset wings were a popular multipurpose item in Cartier's inventory. One of these new-old whimsies could be worn as a brooch or a buckle attached to a black silk or enamel gold chain belt. Cole Porter's wife, Linda, was one of several stylish women who had a Cartier scarab jewel.

Of the many faraway places on Cartier's creative itinerary, the firm returned to India frequently during the twenties and thirties. The land of the Raj provided a bazaar full of ideas, bibs, beads, and decorative terminals—all of these appeared in Cartier designs. For example, Mughal armbands in gold, enamel, and precious stones led Cartier to do its own version in diamonds. Cartier's inspiration for beast head bangles came directly from Jaipur. And a couple of the firm's tiaras looked just like maharani-wear. Barbara Hutton had one with seven emeralds—the largest weighing 100.15 carats—set in a design imitating an Indian mounting for unusually shaped flat Mughal-cut diamonds.

Merle Oberon's Indian-style necklace
by Cartier has diamond rondelles
and twenty-nine rock-size emeralds.

Twentieth Century–Fox production chief Darryl F. Zanuck sits
between Joan Bennett (left) and Merle Oberon, who is wearing her
Cartier emerald bead necklace, at a nightclub in the 1930s.

The Cartier brothers' exotica was a far cry from the court styles of their grandfather, Louis-François Cartier. When he established the Parisian firm in 1847, Louis-François aspired to make jewelry fit for a queen. His first royal client, Princess Mathilde, crossed the threshold in 1856. At the turn of the century, Louis-Francois's son, Alfred (1841–1925), made jewels in the prevailing style of diamonds and platinum with bows, garlands, and swags to perfection. From 1904 to 1920 the firm received ten royal appointments. Monarchs all over the world, including King Edward VI of England, King Alfonso XIII of Spain, Czar Nicholas II of Russia, King George I of Greece, and Victor Emmanuel III of Italy, showered Cartier with commissions. During the 1920s royal appointments dwindled after Alfred Cartier passed away, and his sons began making jewelry that was far too exotic for nobility but perfect for adventurous millionaires.

Fruit salad, a style Cartier launched in the late 1920s, was one of the most delicious on its new menu. The east-meets-west jewelry featured rubies, emeralds, and sapphires carved into leaves and berries by Indian craftsmen. The remarkable blend of precious stones packed into wide bracelets, clip brooches, and bib necklaces whetted the appetite of Cartier's discriminating, untitled celebrity clients. Cole Porter picked up one bracelet in

1926, another in 1930, and a clip brooch in 1935 for his wife Linda. Singer Sewing Machine heiress Daisy Fellowes commissioned a fruit salad necklace in 1936. Other jewelers found fruit salad appetizing as well. Many stole the recipe and tossed their own fruit salad jewels.

Since 1915 the panther, one of the sleekest beasts of the jungle, had been prowling around the Cartier design studio. Panther dots speckled a lapel watch brooch in the early years of the century. A panther lounged in a 1920s advertisement. The cat became the firm's unofficial mascot at mid-century when there was a population explosion of panthers. The first of the new litter preened on a 152-carat cabochon sapphire brooch and belonged to the Duchess of Windsor. Other cats with black onyx or sapphire spots draped themselves over rings, bangles, and brooches. Barbara Hutton and Nina Dyer were just a couple of the women who adopted cats at Cartier in the fifties and sixties.

The imaginative jewelry made under the tenure of the Cartier brothers and artistic director Jeanne Toussaint has proved to be some of the most celebrated of the twentieth century.

The Duchess of Windsor's diamond panther brooch by Cartier has sapphire spots and canary diamond eyes and a 152-carat sapphire orb.

The Duchess of Windsor pinned her Cartier panther brooch to her coat for an event in 1967 at Marlborough House in London.

For a 1934 photo session with Cecil Beaton, Daisy Fellowes boldly combined her Cartier fruit salad necklace with an embroidered jacket by Schiaparelli.

Daisy Fellowes's fruit salad necklace features diamonds, Indian-carved rubies, emeralds, and sapphires. Originally the jewel had a cord on the back, a traditional element in Indian jewelry. It was replaced with gems by Fellowes's daughter, the Countesse de Castilla, in 1963.

Barbara Hutton posed
for photographer Cecil
Beaton in Tangiers
wearing an Indian sari
and her Cartier emerald
necklace as a tiara. The
exotic jewel, made in
1947, features seven
emeralds. The largest is
a 100.15-carat gem
that came from the
collection of Catherine
the Great.

An ancient Egyptian scarab is the centerpiece of a brooch made by Cartier in 1925. The jewel takes flight with wings of diamonds and half-moon shape emeralds, as well as knife-shape citrines, topaz, rubies, and onyx specially cut to look like feathers.

There have been numerous museum exhibitions staged around the world commemorating this era. A shelf full of books focusing on Cartier's golden years have been written. And the historical, exotic designs led by the panther have been a big source of inspiration for the firm's design studio.

ESTABLISHED: 1847

FOUNDER: Louis-François Cartier (1819–1904)

SELECT BOOKS: Nadelhoffer, Hans. *Cartier, Jewelers Extraordinary*. New York: Harry N. Abrams, 1984; Rudoe, Judy. *Cartier 1900–1939*. Exhibition catalogue. New York: Harry N. Abrams and The Metropolitan Museum of Art, 1997; Trétiack, Philippe. *Cartier*. New York: Universe Publishing, 1997.

A FEW OF THE EXHIBITIONS: 1997, New York. *Cartier 1900–1939*. The Metropolitan Museum of Art, The British Museum; 1989, Paris. *The Art of Cartier*. Paris Musée du Petit Palais, 1992, St. Petersburg Hermitage Museum; 1982, Los Angeles. *Retrospective Louis Cartier: Masterworks of Art Deco*. Los Angeles County Museum of Art.

SOME MOVIE CREDITS: *'Til We Meet Again* (1940), *Lifeboat* (1944), *Stage Fright* (1950), *Sunset Boulevard* (1950), *Star!* (1968), *The Getaway* (1972), *The Exorcist* (1973), *The Great Gatsby* (1974), *A Little Night Music* (1978), *French Kiss* (1995)

LOCATIONS: Cartier has over 185 stores in about 123 countries. The flagship is in Paris.

VAN CLEEF & ARPELS

Among the displays of geometric jewels at the 1925 Exposition des Art Décoratifs et Industriales Modernes in Paris, Van Cleef & Arpels showed jewels with rose motifs. The firm made the rose modern by flattening out the flower on the surface of a wide bracelet and pumping up its color. Rubies and diamonds defined the petals, canary diamonds marked the pistils, emeralds tinted the leaves, black onyx filled in the stems, and rubies made prickly thorns.

Van Cleef's Roaring Twenties rose bracelet won a grand prize at the exhibition. It also kicked off the glory days of the French firm that lasted from the twenties to the fifties when a number of the members of the Van Cleef and Arpels families worked together. Alfred Van Cleef was in essence the director of operations and strategist. He made sure the firm was a place where art and jewelry went hand in hand. Julien Arpels had an eye for gems and was responsible for many major gem purchases. Charles and Louis Arpels (1886–1976) were salesmen who hustled. Estelle Van Cleef, Alfred's wife and the Arpels sister, kept the books balanced. And Alfred Van Cleef's daughter, Renée Puissant (1897–1942) was the art director from 1926 to 1942. After Puissant passed away, her legacy was carried on by designer Maurice Duvalet who wasn't a member of either family, but he perfectly understood the family's refined and elegant sensibility.

During the forties Louis Arpels's passion for ballet and dance was captured by Duvalet in a collection of ballerina brooches made up of large old-fashioned rose-cut diamonds, emeralds, and rubies. The dancers in the series were not an anonymous troop; they were marquee names from the history of ballet. Eighteenth-century French dancer Maria Camargo starred in several brooches. For authenticity and detail, Duvalet studied a portrait of the ballerina by Nicolas Lancret. A publicity photograph of Anna Pavlova, dipping into a curtsy after a performance of *Coppelia*

Six roses in rubies, diamonds, emeralds, and black onyx decorate a wide bracelet made by Van Cleef & Arpels in 1925.

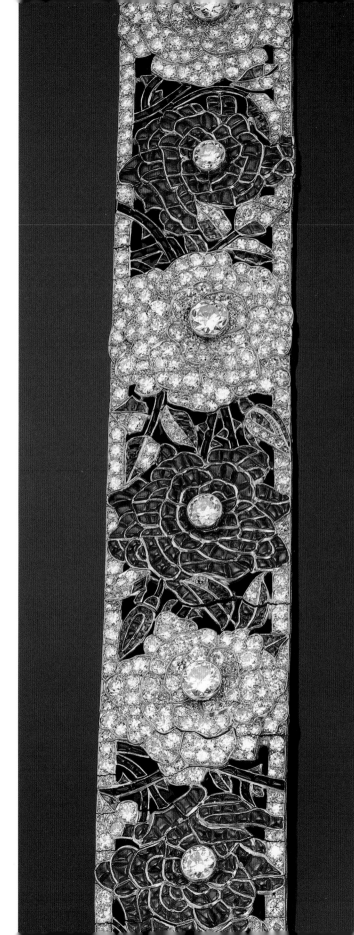

on her 1910 American tour, was Duvalet's source for his brooches of the Russian ballerina. A corps of loyal American balletomanes, including Marjorie Merriweather Post and Mrs. Woolworth Donahue, pirouetted away with these jewels.

Van Cleef & Arpels's ultimate design achievement was invisibly-set jewels, pieces with settings concealed under a blanket of gems. Similar to couture, where hundreds of hours go into making a dress—beading, embroidering, and carefully fitting it to a client's body—hundreds of hours went into every invisibly-set piece. Each gem had to be specially cut into squares and parallelograms, customized with grooves on the back in order to fit on a fine metal track in the setting. None of the gems could be recycled and used again in another jewel because of the way they were cut. The resale value of the gems was sacrificed for the design. Generally, rubies and sapphires were the gems of choice for this tricky technique. Emeralds were too soft to be grooved, and diamonds too hard, although Van Cleef made at least one invisibly-set diamond leaf brooch.

Other firms, including Cartier, Verdura, the American manufacturer Oscar Heyman, and Augusto Iberti, made invisibly-set jewels. In fact Cartier took out a patent for the technique in 1933, the same year Van Cleef filed for its patent. Van Cleef & Arpels, however, was the only jeweler to stick with the invisible setting and fully develop the artistic possibilities. Rings, necklaces, brooches, earrings, and bracelets, as well as cufflinks, compacts, lipstick cases, and mascara boxes were covered with invisibly-set gems by Van Cleef & Arpels. First Lady of Argentina Eva Perón displayed her patriotism with an invisibly-set brooch of her nation's flag. The firm also used the invisible style of setting in a special commission jewel for Jules Bache, the American financier and art collector, who wanted a gem-set copy of his Goya painting, *The Red Boy*. Van Cleef captured the spirit of the work of art in a brooch of the boy suited up in invisibly-set rubies and coifed with invisibly-set blue sapphire hair. Bache gave the little jewelry masterpiece to his daughter, American socialite and best-dressed-list favorite, Mrs. Gilbert Miller.

Van Cleef & Arpels stayed with its formal way of doing things throughout the twentieth century. The design repertoire of refined artistic subjects and fancy floral themes has been consistently a part of the Van Cleef & Arpels design philosophy over the decades. New invisibly-set showpieces are made by the firm regularly. In 1992 at the Musée de la Mode et du Costume exhibition of Van

A Maria Camargo ballerina brooch (right) with rose-cut diamonds, rubies, and emeralds made by Van Cleef & Arpels in 1942. The brooch belonged to Marjorie Merriweather Post.

An Anna Pavlova ballerina brooch (left) with rose-cut diamonds, emeralds, and rubies made by Van Cleef & Arpels.

Barbara Hutton in her Van Cleef & Arpels ballerina brooch sits with her son Lance Reventlow and goddaughter Diana Kennerley.

A Wings of Victory brooch made by Van Cleef & Arpels in 1944 to celebrate the liberation of Paris.

One of several drawings done by Van Cleef & Arpels around 1942 for a special commission brooch of the Goya painting, *The Red Boy*.

Cleef & Arpels in Paris, some of the year's most extravagant invisibly-set jewels sat alongside invisibly-set jewels made in the thirties.

ESTABLISHED: 1906
FOUNDERS: Alfred Van Cleef (1873–1938) and his brothers-in-law Charles (1880–1951) and Julien Arpels (1884–1964)
BOOK: Raulet, Sylvie. *Van Cleef & Arpels*. New York: Rizzoli, 1987.
EXHIBITIONS: 1992, Paris. *Van Cleef & Arpels*. Musée de la Mode et du Costume; 1990, Los Angeles. *A Jeweler's Art: Masterpieces from Van Cleef & Arpels*. Los Angeles County Museum of Art, The Smithsonian Institution, Washington, D. C., Honolulu Academy of the Arts.
MOVIE CREDIT: *The Last Metro* (1980)
LOCATIONS: Van Cleef & Arpels has about 11 branches in 6 countries. The flagship is in Paris.

From the 1930s to the 50s, Van Cleef & Arpels made several holly leaf brooches with invisibly-set rubies, pavè-set diamonds and baguette-cut diamond stems. This 1950s version of the brooch belonged to Enid Haupt, editor-in-chief of *Seventeen*.

The Duchess of Windsor wore her holly leaf brooch to a Broadway show in 1941.

HARRY WINSTON

"Nicolas Cage and Susan Sarandon win top acting Oscars," announced the *New York Times* in 1996, but the headlines might just as well have read, "Harry Winston sweeps the Academy Awards." Twenty-nine stars sailed down the red carpet in Winston jewelry that year. At the head of the diamond parade were Mira Sorvino and Angela Bassett. Elegant is the word for Sorvino's necklace with 110 carats worth of diamonds set in a delicate ray pattern. Megawatts describes Bassett's 273-carat diamond necklace that sent out shock waves with its high-voltage glamour. The astonishing collar had a double row of pear and brilliant-cut diamonds, twenty-three pendants featuring two marquise, a pear, and a brilliant-cut diamond, and five super-large pendants of square-cut diamonds, garnished by marquise and pear-shape diamonds. With a price tag of $6.5 million, this jewel was the big-budget blockbuster of the evening.

Harry Winston, the flamboyant founder of the firm, would have enjoyed the 1996 Oscars. The evening had everything he liked. Winston adored Hollywood stars. He had always understood their lure. In 1934, two years after Winston established the firm, he put Shirley Temple, one of the biggest box office draws of the early thirties, under contract. The child star posed for publicity photographs with Winston's prize acquisition, the 726-carat Jonker diamond, the second largest rough diamond in the world. Harry Winston would have loved the fact that millions of viewers tuned in to the Oscars and saw the firm's jewelry.

The last place Winston wanted to keep his precious gems was in the vaults of his Fifth Avenue store. He frequently loaned jewelry to *Vogue* and *Harper's Bazaar* for cover shoots and major editorial spreads. So the public could see important jewelry live, Winston toured his collection of gems and jewels, called the "Court of Jewels," as far afield as Europe, Cuba, and the Texas State Fair for over ten years from the late forties to the mid-fifties. The 44.5-carat Hope Diamond—made famous by its curse, inky blue color, and royal French provenance—and the 44.63- and 44.18-carat Indore Pears—two diamonds of exactly the same color and almost exactly the same size from the Maharajah of Indore's personal jewelry box—were headliners in the collection. Above all else on Oscar night, Harry Winston would have loved the razzle-dazzle jewelry worn by the actresses. He had made his name on jewels with huge total-carat weights presented in graceful designs.

A holly wreath necklace made by Harry Winston in 1961 has 128 marquise, pear, and circular-cut diamonds weighing approximately 168-carats. The jewel, which belonged to Caroline Ryan Foulke, can be divided and worn as two bracelets.

Life illustrated a 1952 article on Harry Winston with a photograph of the jeweler hidden in the shadows of his New York office. Winston's insurance company did not want his face to be photographed and seen by potential jewelry thieves because of the $10-million value of his Court of Jewels collection.

During the fifty-plus years Winston ran his firm, he searched for new ways to showcase diamonds on necklaces, bracelets, and earrings. Winston did not care for informal jewelry. All the firm's designs were gem-laden. The "C" Scroll, a Winston signature earring design, was an adroit concept for a small handful of gems. Three lines of brilliant-cut diamonds looped from the front to the back of the ear.

Slightly over 24 carats of circular-cut diamonds make up these "C" scroll earrings by Harry Winston.

Winston himself came up with the idea for the holly wreath setting, the firm's most famous design, one year around Christmas when he was looking at the wreath on the door of his house. He thought the points of the leaves and the round berries looked like marquise, pear, and brilliant-cut diamonds. With the image in mind, Winston went to his atelier which was fully staffed with a designer, lapidary, stone-setters, and gem cutters, and told them about his brainstorm. Together they translated the concept from nature into jewelry. The gems, set in an orderly jumble on platinum wire mounts, made up the signature setting.

Winston's crowning design achievement attracted clients with deep pockets like Caroline Ryan Foulke, granddaughter of the New York businessman Thomas Fortune Ryan. Foulke had two holly wreath necklaces—one with 168 carats of diamonds and the other with 149.19 carats of diamonds. The Duchess of Windsor owned a holly wreath brooch. Her piece was made in 1956 and it had 38.73 carats of diamonds.

The Harry Winston firm has never gone to0 far away from its founder's emphasis on big-time diamond jewelry. Unlike many other large jewelry firms that have created less expensive boutique lines, Winston makes only prestige jewelry, magnificent, block-buster pieces with important gems that turn up on Hollywood stars at the Oscars. Although there has never been a museum exhibition devoted to the jewelry of Harry Winston, the firm has left a part of its legacy to the Smithsonian. Beginning in 1958, Winston donated several gems, including the famed Hope Diamond, to the institution. Harry's son Ronald Winston, who took over the firm in 1978 when his father died, made a major donation to the Smithsonian in the early 1990s. The money was used toward a complete renovation of the gem hall and a special gallery named after Harry Winston. The centerpiece of the Winston gallery is the Hope Diamond.

ESTABLISHED: 1932
FOUNDER: Harry Winston (1896–1978)
SELECT BOOKS: Krashes, Laurence. *Harry Winston: The Ultimate Jeweler*. Santa Monica: Gemological Institute of America, 1984; Gregory, Alexis. *Harry Winston: Rare Jewels of the World*. New York: Universe Publishing, 1998.
SOME MOVIE CREDITS: *What a Way to Go!* (1964), *The Graduate* (1967), *Everybody Says I Love You* (1997)
LOCATIONS: New York, Beverly Hills, Paris, Geneva, Tokyo, Osaka

BULGARI

At the dawn of the disco era, Bulgari boogied like no other jeweler. During the late sixties and seventies, jet-set women danced the night away with Bulgari coin-chains swinging or bright Bulgari gemmy jewelry catching the strobe lights. Richard Burton gave Elizabeth Taylor several jewels from Bulgari during this time. "I introduced her to beer," said Burton. "And she introduced me to Bulgari." Pop artist Andy Warhol collected Bulgari jewelry. "When I'm in Rome I always visit Bulgari," said Warhol, "because it is the most important museum of contemporary art." The appearance of Bulgari jewelry on the cover of Andy Warhol's magazine *Interview,* a bellwether of cool, was perhaps the best indicator of its popularity among the young, wealthy, famous, and glamorous. Bianca Jagger and Jessica Lange were just two of the celebrity cover girls who showed up in big, bold Bulgari baubles.

The Bulgari brothers were as young, if not younger, than their clientele when they took charge of the firm in 1964. The oldest, Gianni, was 29, Paolo was 27, and Nicola was 23. Together they electrified the firm by making jewelry for their generation. "People are looking for amusement," said Gianni Bulgari in a 1970s interview. "They no longer want something they put on or carry for great occasions, but jewelry they wear often with many things."

Bulgari reacted to fashion almost as quickly as clothing designers. The Star Spangled Banner Collection shows how with-it the firm was. The line had hoop earrings and neckwires with disc-shaped pendants, looks synonymous with the swinging seventies. Bulgari's rearranged stars and stripes that decorated the jewelry were made in coral, diamonds, and lapis.

Elizabeth Taylor dropped by Bulgari on a 1967 shopping spree in Rome.

The Bulgari brothers, Nicola, Gianni, and Paolo (from left to right), transformed the family firm into an international enterprise in the 1970s.

Bulgari infused pared-down, blown-up gold, and diamond jewelry with colors that were every bit as loud as seventies clothes. There was a generous supply of black, yellow, red, and blue enamel in Bulgariland. A diamond and yellow enamel snake bracelet is one dramatic example of Bulgari's way with color. Not only is yellow enamel shellacked all over the coils, but it is super-charged with an underlayer of textured gold, and lit up with patches of diamonds.

Bulgari meshed its old-world Greek and Roman heritage into its modern jewelry repertoire. Nicola Bulgari, who was a coin collector, came up with the idea of updating the concept of coin jewelry. In the third century AD, Romans wore gold rings with a gold coin depicting Emperor Caracalla. Old coins mounted in new jewelry were also popular in the nineteenth century, when women wore silver Greek coins from the fourth century BC, which were mounted in detailed filigree frames on gold bracelets. Bulgari's take on the look was to mount the antique coins in basic gold link chains with diamond accents. Lyn Revson, wife of Charles Revson of Revlon, had a small collection of classical coins in one Bulgari necklace that she wore casually with a turtleneck and designer jeans. The 18-carat yellow and white gold necklace had ten silver coins from Corinth dating from the 4th to the 3rd century BC. They all showed the head of the goddess of wisdom, Athena, on one side, and the winged horse of heroes, Pegasus, on the other.

One of the most significant things the Bulgari brothers did throughout the seventies was open branches in major cities and hot vacationing spots for the jet-set. In 1971 Bulgari made its New York debut, followed up by branch openings in Geneva in 1974, Monte Carlo in 1977, and Paris in 1979. This was an explosion of activity for the ninety-year-old Roman institution.

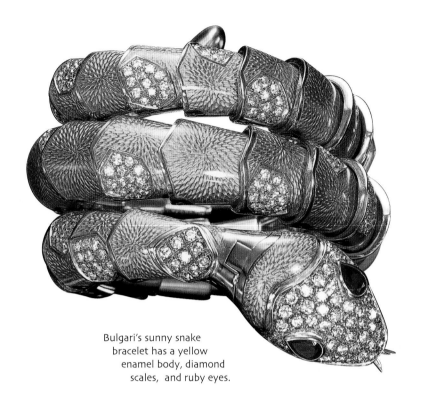

Bulgari's sunny snake bracelet has a yellow enamel body, diamond scales, and ruby eyes.

The first Bulgari shop was set up in Rome in 1884 by Sotirio Bulgari, a Greek immigrant from Corfu and the Bulgari brothers' grandfather. Around this time the firm sold jewelry with a Roman look, mementos for wealthy Americans and European aristocracy on their grand tours of Italy. By the 1920s Sotirio and his sons Giorgio (1890–1966), father of the Bulgari brothers, and Costantino (1889–1973) all worked at the firm's lavish store on the Via Condotti. Gemmy and geometric Art Deco wide bracelets, clip brooches, pendant earrings, and necklaces made up the inventory. The jewels had lots of fancy-cut diamonds, squared edges, and blocks of color defined by faceted and big cabochon gems. Bulgari's Art Deco jewelry was streamlined and glamorous with few exotic details. Though the designs were adept—they attract-ed Hollywood stars Mary Pickford and Gary Cooper as well as New York socialites Florence Gould, Clare Boothe Luce, and Brooke Astor—they weren't strikingly original. The jewels could have been produced by any good jeweler of the era.

The designs made by Bulgari in the late sixties and seventies could not be mistaken for any other jeweler. They were original. The first thing that hits you about the high-end pieces—the bibs and the 26-inch-long necklaces with large pendants— is the sophisticated color palette. In one stunning necklace Bulgari blended rubies, emeralds, and sapphires with robin's egg blue

THE SEXY BEAT OF CHER

66 ...I got you,
you wear my ring 99

Contemporary flash: modern girl, modern jewels—
Cher and Bulgari's stars and stripes of coral, diamonds, lapis—
real, but not too serious even for the simple little
jersey bathing suits here. And that's the whole point about
today's jewelry—it's to wear, to use, to enjoy....
A great red-and-black maillot, left,
wrapped like a surplice, tied in back; $32. With a sunburst pendant
and earrings....Small squared-off trunks, right—
this year's bikini look ($28), with a neck-chain worn as a belt,
a ring in the same stars-and-stripes pattern.
The jewels, from the Star Spangled Banner
Collection by Bulgari-Danaos,
Hotel Pierre. Bathing suits by Eres;
nylon and Lycra. Bloomingdale's.

A *Vogue* fashion spread of Cher wearing several pieces from Bulgari's Star Spangled Banner collection with a bathing suit captured the casual state of the nation in 1972.

35

Two gold necklaces by Bulgari featuring old coins from ancient Rome (top) and Greece.

turquoise, brown sugar colored citrines, and deep purple amethysts. Most of the gems in this necklace and many others were cabochons. The shape fit Bulgari's design philosophy. A faceted stone can be hard and formal, whereas a cabochon tends to be softer and more artistic.

The policy of making modern jewelry, things that aren't nostalgic but right for contemporary fashion, is something Bulgari has stuck by since the seventies. When jewelry historians Daniela Mascetti and Amanda Triossi approached the firm about writing a book on its history, Paolo and Nicola Bulgari said, "We were afraid that digging into the past to find our roots would have infringed a fundamental rule we have always tried to follow: to look ahead, to think of the future and to innovate, revolutionize, and modernize." The Bulgaris agreed to do the book, after some reflection, realizing that the firm's past was "perhaps, directly correlated to our present." Though collections and styles have changed at the firm, elements of the youthful seventies jewelry have been maintained. Jewels with semiprecious cabochons and ancient coins are perennial favorites. The seventies is also still alive in the way Bulgari throws a party. At the reopening of its New York store in 1997 after a period of renovation, Bulgari did not have a black tie gala. Instead, the store became a disco for one night with DJ Boy George presiding over the turntables, red velvet ropes at the door, and laser lights flashing inside and out. The house was packed with late nineties jet-setters.

ESTABLISHED: 1884

FOUNDER: Sotirio Bulgari (1857–1932)

BOOK: Mascetti, Daniela and Amanda Triossi. *Bulgari*. Milan: Leonardo Arte Srl, 1996.

SOME MOVIE CREDITS: *King Kong* (1976), *Reversal of Fortune* (1990), *Prêt-à-Porter* (1994), *Casino* (1995), *Waiting to Exhale* (1995), *First Wives Club* (1996), *Evita* (1996), *The End of Violence* (1997), and *The Thomas Crown Affair* (1999).

LOCATIONS: Bulgari has over 64 branches in 24 countries. The flagship is in Rome.

A tour-de-force 26-inch-long necklace by Bulgari shows a harmonious blend of colorful gems. Links of small cabochon sapphires connect to links of small flame-colored cabochon citrines, which connect to links of spring green emeralds. The scalloped shield-shape diamond pendant boasts a big pear-shape cabochon emerald and little round cabochon sapphires and pear-shape cabochon citrines.

THE AESTHETES

René Lalique created the first new look in twentieth-century jewelry. The original style did not happen by chance, nor was it something that slowly evolved for the innovative designer. He had some hurtles to jump before he could leave the mainstream jewelry industry he had been a part of all his professional life. During an interview with jewelry historian Henri Vever, Lalique explained, "It was important to me to put in a considerable amount of work to make jewelry that was different from anything that had been done before." He continued, "I made an extraordinary push to leave behind everything I had previously done."

The theatrical style Lalique invented was replete with vivid imagery—maidens and monsters, heroes, and lovers kissing. There were fairy-tale scenes from nature, chill winter landscapes, serene swan-filled lakes, and romantic sunsets over mountain tops. The fantasy world he depicted in his pendants, brooches, bracelets, necklaces, and combs sprang to life in a sophisticated blend of enamels and semiprecious gems.

Lalique's style (briefly called Genre Lalique before it was assimilated into the decorative arts movement named Art Nouveau) inspired many other jewelers, including Vever and Georges Fouquet. The official French jewelry association, the Chambre Syndicale de la Bijouterie, de la Joaillerie et de l'Orfèvrerie, threw their weight behind Lalique's new style, which caused a sensation at the 1900 Paris Exposition Universelle.

The reign of Art Nouveau, however, did not last long. During the peak of its success in the early 1900s, the works of great Art Nouveau jewelers were knocked off and mass-produced by lesser designers. Imitations lacking fine craftsmanship flooded the market and contributed to the demise of Art Nouveau jewelry around 1910.

LALIQUE

René Lalique, the most admired Art Nouveau jewelry designer, worshipped by the critics and his peers, had a hard time selling his new style in the beginning. He told Vever, "I chose to exhibit at the Salon because whenever I presented my pieces to the most prestigious stores, I was annoyed to hear them smile and say,

A watercolor of René Lalique at his work table surrounded with some of his sources of inspiration.

'Very pretty, charming. Oh! That is very pleasing to us, but it will not please our clients.'" Lalique's jewelry was daring and definitely a commercial risk. Everything from snakes and swans to nuns and naked revelers; from half-woman, half-dragonfly creatures to half-woman, half-flower charmers was in the mix.

Lalique's break with the establishment came in 1895 when he premiered his new jewelry at the Paris Exposition sponsored by the Société des Artistes Française. Before that he had logged fifteen years in the traditional fine-jewelry industry beginning as a jeweler's apprentice in 1880. Five years later, at age twenty-five,

The Winter Landscape pendant, designed by Lalique around 1900, has an enamel scene of freshly fallen snow in the forest, framed in gold boughs with marquise-cut blue glass pine cones and a pear-shape gray pearl.

A procession of nuns go down the center of an enamel plaque designed by Lalique around 1900. The pendant is suspended from a black enamel and gold chain.

he owned his own workshop, which turned out diamond designs in the popular court style for jewelers including Boucheron, Cartier, and Tiffany.

At the 1895 exposition, Lalique became the darling of the Paris avant-garde. Sarah Bernhardt commissioned him to do jewelry for her stage performances and personal jewelry box. The trendsetting Madame Meurlot-Chollet was also a devotee. On the international exhibition circuit, a forum where jewelers were awarded for creativity, Lalique was a big winner. At the 1900 Paris Exposition, Lalique and Vever shared the grand prize. This triumph was followed by a victory lap of expositions in Turin (1902), Berlin (1903), and London (1903). When Lalique debuted his work in the American midwest at the 1904 St. Louis Exposition, he acquired several American clients with unconventional taste including art collector Henry Walters from Baltimore, who purchased nine pieces, and President Theodore Roosevelt's daughter, the independent and fashion-forward Alice Roosevelt.

Sarah Bernhardt, Lalique's most famous patron, wears an enamel pendant with swans among her numerous long chains.

The Narcisse gold dog collar plaque by Lalique features two enamel figures surrounded by blue and green enamel chrysanthemums.

Lalique decorated his display area at the 1900 Paris Exposition with his bronze sculptures of nude women with large wings draped in sheer fabric. Henri Vever's comparatively modest case is to the right.

Lalique's gold, enamel, and opal iris bracelet was exhibited at the Paris Salon in 1897 and the 1900 Paris Exposition.

What wowed the crowds at exhibitions in Europe and America were the unusual and moody aesthetics of Lalique jewels. His iris bracelet, an award-winning piece at the 1900 exposition, is a perfect example of his magnetic work. The bracelet features five soulful blue enamel irises growing along gold whiplash lines. Curling and drooping petals set a turbulent mood and make the flowers appear to be on the verge of death. Large-cut opals are the backdrop for this little melodrama.

A pendant Lalique designed around the time of the St. Louis Exposition illustrates how he told, or rather suggested, a story in a jewel. The piece pairs a frame of two intertwined enamel cobras

A gold pocket watch by Lalique conjures up the story of Bram Stoker's *Dracula*, the best-selling 1897 novel. On the face, light blue-and-white enamel butterflies flutter as symbols of dawn: on the back, dark blue enamel bats swoop around moonstones. A gold serpent, the emblem of eternity, presides over the scene, coiled around the wind stem.

Sculptor Madame Meurlot-Chollet poses in
Lalique's Princesse Lointaine pendant.

and a glass cameo of a nude female holding out a transparent
scarf (see page 10, right). Oscar Wilde's scandalous 1893 *Salome* is
a possible source of inspiration. The sultry female could easily be
the play's leading lady, and the snakes a metaphor for her evil
mind and deeds. Another candidate for the jewel's inspiration is
Cleopatra in her enchantress mode, about to seduce Mark
Anthony. The story was popular at the time due to a big Sarah
Bernhardt production. The snake frame could allude to Cleopatra's
cobra crown and the poisonous asp she used to commit suicide.
Although the drapery of the jewel's protagonist is classical, her hair-
style is turn-of-the century, making it difficult to decipher which
historical character she might be.

Lalique held his last jewelry exhibition in 1912, but it was far
from the end of his professional life. In 1913, at age fifty-three, he

purchased a glass factory and began an illustrious second career.
Lalique's designs for glass vases, objects, and other assorted items
are manufactured by the firm that bears his name to this day. In
fact, the popularity of Lalique's glass designs have eclipsed his triumph in Art Nouveau jewelry.

DATES: René Lalique began exhibiting his jewelry in 1895. He sold
his jewelry on the exhibition circuit and at some retail establishments such as Samuel Bing's gallery L'Art Nouveau. He opened a
store in 1905.
FOUNDER: René Lalique (1860–1945)
SELECT BOOKS: Barten, Sigrid. *René Lalique, Schmuck und Objets
d'Art 1890–1910.* Munich: Prestel-Verlag, 1977; Brunhammer,
Yvonne, ed. *The Jewels of Lalique.* Exhibition Catalogue. New
York: Flammarion, 1998; *René Lalique: Jewelry, Glass. Exhibition
catalogue.* Paris: Musée des Arts Decoratifs, Réunion des musées
nationaux, 1991.
A FEW OF THE EXHIBITIONS: 2000, Yokohama. *René Lalique
1860–1945.* Sogo Museum of Art Yokohama, Tokyo Metropolitan
Teien Museum, Kyoto National Museum of Art; 1998, New York.
The Jewels of Lalique. Cooper-Hewitt, National Design Museum,
Washington, D. C., Smithsonian Institution, Dallas Museum of
Art; 1991, Paris. *René Lalique, Jewelry Glass.* Musée des Art
Decoratifs, Tokyo, The National Museum of Modern Art; 1987,
London. *The Jewellery of René Lalique;* 1985 Baltimore. *Art
Nouveau Jewelry by René Lalique.* Baltimore. The Walters Art
Gallery; 1978, Zurich. *René Lalique.* Museum Bellerive.
LOCATIONS: Lalique has approximately 40 boutiques in 16 coun-
tries. The flagship is in Paris.

FOUQUET

When the Parisian jeweler Georges Fouquet (1862–1957)
convinced Sarah Bernhardt's creative director Alphonse Mucha to
design a boutique and collaborate on jewelry for the 1900 Paris
Exposition, he nabbed someone whose style was the personification
of Art Nouveau at its most extravagant. Mucha's designs at the
exposition drew mobs of people to Fouquet's case. One of the
biggest attractions was Mucha's snake bracelet for Sarah Bernhardt,
an enamel concoction extending from the elbow to the wrist with
chains attached to a huge ring in the shape of a crab. The second
part of Mucha's association with Fouquet was just as much of a

crowd pleaser. Mucha's sensuous Art Nouveau boutique seduced clients into its otherworldly interior and made the viewing of Fouquet's jewelry a mind-altering experience. The clients let go of their previous notions as to what jewelry should or should not be and slipped into the style's intoxicating mood.

Fouquet's passion for Art Nouveau had been ignited in 1895, the year he saw Lalique's first jewelry exhibition and the year he took the reins of the family business from his father. Awestruck by the changing jewelry landscape, Fouquet began to switch the firm's inventory from his father's revivalist collections to the new style. His flamboyant jewels quickly earned him the reputation as the showman of Art Nouveau.

The Fouquet flair for drama is perfectly illustrated in a Chinese dragon corsage brooch, one of a series of 7¾-inch-long jewels that were the same shape and size as the elongated triangular diamond and platinum bodice brooches popular around 1900. But that is where the similarities end. Fouquet's corsage brooch is a mythical monster with a dark and light green enamel serpentine body snapped into a whiplash line. Mottled brown plique-à-jour enamel wings extend from the beast's moss agate and emerald-studded neck. The gold head and jaws clamp onto a pendant gold seaweed motif accented by green enamel sprays with pink freshwater pearl buds. A large pear-shaped pearl anchors the design.

With his sophisticated antennae for change, Georges Fouquet moved on when the fashion for Art Nouveau was over at the end of the first decade of the twentieth century. At a 1910 exhibition in Brussels, Fouquet showed a new style of work where the enamel was subsidiary to the stylized gem motifs. His display included gemmy circular pendants and a plique-à-jour bandeau with large diamond, pearl, and aquamarine flowers. These jewels were part of the transition to Art Deco, the next big wave in design.

DATES: 1862–1936
FOUNDER: Alphonse Fouquet (1828–1911)
LOCATION: Paris
BOOK: *Les Fouquet. Exhibition catalogue.* Paris: Musée des Art Décoratifs, 1983.
EXHIBITION: 1983, Paris. *Les Fouquet.* Musée des Art Décoratifs. Zurich Museum Bellerive.

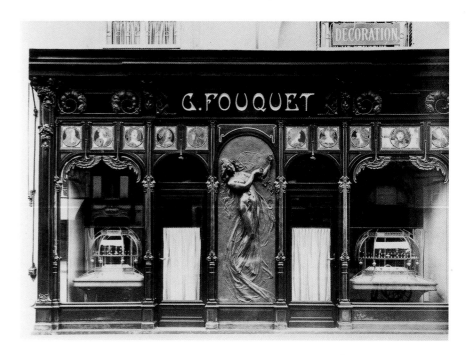

The Fouquet storefront, designed by Alphonse Mucha, featured a ten-foot-tall bronze sculpture of an alluring woman offering jewelry to passers-by on the rue Royale.

Inside the Fouquet boutique there was a sculpture of a peacock projecting from one wall, and a fountain of a nude with little dragons at her feet on another wall.

Georges Fouquet won a gold medal at the Art Nouveau Paris Exposition for his firm's work.

In a Birth of Venus pendant by Fouquet, an ivory statuette of the love goddess stands in a champlevé enamel and gold setting with a yellow shell, red branch coral, green seaweed, and a blue arch. The piece, made in 1900, has a pearl drop and a yellow gold chain.

Opposite: A plique-à-jour enamel pendant brooch and chain by Fouquet accented with turquoise, diamonds, and a baroque pearl.

The Chinese dragon in Fouquet's corsage brooch made in 1902 is composed of plique-à-jour enamel. Moss agate, emeralds, pink freshwater pearls, and a baroque pearl accent the gold work in the design.

VEVER

In 1898 Henri Vever (1853–1942) wrote in his diary, "I am convinced that we are in a very rare period, I should say unique, for the production of new types of jewelry. Everyone is saturated, disgusted, nauseated to see the repetition of the hackneyed jewelry in the style of Louis XV." Looking optimistically to the future, he added, "No matter what, one really wants new things. A new style of jewelry is beginning to appear. The movement is taking shape with an extraordinary rapidity, especially in the last two or three years."

One of the most enthusiastic supporters of the Art Nouveau style he alluded to in his diary, Vever not only became an Art Nouveau jeweler himself, he also spent a lot of time writing about the achievements of other Art Nouveau jewelers such as Fouquet, Lucien Gaillard, and Gabriel Falguières for his book, *Histoire de la Bijouterie Française au XIXe Siecle,* published in 1908. The last pages of the three-volume publication were preserved for his favorite—Lalique. Vever wrote, "[Lalique] has without a doubt made the greatest contribution to the revitalization of jewelry in our time."

As much as Vever admired Lalique, however, the family firm he ran with his brother Paul (1850–1915) did not follow the father of Art Nouveau jewelry into the realm of hybrid female monsters, nightmarish dream sequences, and eroticism. Comparatively, the subjects of Vever's jewels were tame. The plants and flowers in Vever's field guide to nature have no thorns. Delicate green enamel mistletoe leaves with pearl berry accents wind around the top of a Vever horn hair comb. The blooms and stem of a slender and drooping Fuchsia shrub form a languid enamel and diamond pendant.

The women in Vever jewels have peaceful souls. Omphale, the queen of Lydia who disarmed Hercules through beauty and love, is the centerpiece of a sweet bib necklace showing a gold and enamel depiction of the gentle heroine, au naturel, toting the hero's club. Her supporting cast of characters are two gold cupids with opal-studded wings and ruby-tipped arrows. In a gold pendant called Perfume, a young girl holds an oversize flower to her face and sniffs the fragrance.

Vever's charming jewels made the firm successful on the exhibition circuit. It shared the grand prize with Lalique at the 1900 Paris Exposition and both Paul and Henri were recipients of France's highest award, the Legion d'Honneur. Critics liked Vever's work not only because it was masterfully crafted—its top designers René Rozet and Eugene Grasset were major Art

Henri Vever painting in 1895.

Nouveau talents—but also because it was easier to digest than some other jewelers' provocative designs. Jewelry critic Roger Marx said in a review of the 1900 exhibition, "Henri Vever appears to be the goldsmith destined to establish the transition between the old and new schools, between stone setting and decorative jewelry, Mr. Massin [a jeweler who made traditional designs] and Mr. Lalique."

Young girls of the Brittany coast wearing traditional dress were the subject of a series that contributed to Vever winning the grand prize at the 1900 Paris Exposition. Bretons were a popular theme among turn-of-the-century French writers and painters because the fishing villages of Brittany remained relatively untouched by the industrial revolution and were viewed as quaint and picturesque. Vever's masterful rendition of a Breton was an opal, gold, amethyst, and enamel pendant bust of a young girl with a serene expression.

In 1908, the year Vever published his book, the firm moved into new quarters at 14 rue de la Paix. Around the same time Vever, like other jewelers, abandoned Art Nouveau, which was fading in popularity. The firm began to create designs with the fashionable new metal, platinum, which had replaced silver for formal diamond jewels. In 1921 Vever turned the firm over to his nephews, Paul's sons, André and Pierre. The young Vever brothers made a splash and won a grand prize at the 1925 Paris Exposition with an imaginative wide diamond bracelet depicting an Islamic battle scene in colorful enamels and gems. The design paid homage to Henri Vever, who was a collector of Islamic manuscripts. After this tremendous achievement, the Vever brothers maintained a level of quality in the firm's jewelry, but they did not exhibit original jewelry on par with the firm's award-winning designs ever again.

DATES: 1821–1982
FOUNDER: Pierre Vever (1795–1853)
BOOK: Lowry, Glenn D. with Susan Nemazee. *A Jeweler's Eye: Islamic Arts of the Book From the Vever Collection.* Exhibition catalogue. Seattle: University of Washington Press, 1988.
EXHIBITION: 1988, Washington, D. C. *A Jeweler's Eye: Islamic Arts of the Book From the Vever Collection.* The Smithsonian Institution, Arthur M. Sackler Gallery.
LOCATION: Paris

A long drooping diamond stem in a pendant by Vever guides the eye from the plique-à-jour enamel leaves down to the dangling opal flower heads.

A young Breton in a Vever pendant from 1900 wears an opal and diamond bonnet with ribbons that swirl around and form a frame decorated with green and orange enamel stalks of broom, a seaside shrub. The girl's dress has a diamond and gold ruffle that swoops around her shoulder and an amethyst sleeve cut to look like puckered fabric.

THE ROCK HOUNDS

I n the late nineteenth century George Frederick Kunz made gemology a hot topic in America. *The Curious Lore of Precious Gems, Gems and Precious Stones of America,* and *The Book of the Pearls* are three of his gemological treatises that were considered popular reading. Kunz took his show on the road to Europe when he introduced American gems to continental crowds at the 1887 Paris Exposition with a dazzling display he put together for Tiffany & Co. Afterward the entire collection was purchased by J. P. Morgan for the American Museum of Natural History in New York City where the gems went on permanent display.

Kunz's exciting work and the abundance of colorful gems on the market at the turn of the century, such as grass-green demantoid garnets from Russia, pink conch pearls from the Gulf of Mexico and the Indian Ocean, the finest black opals (which are actually dark blue in color) from Lighting Ridge, Australia, white opals from Hungary, and orangish fire opals from Mexico, turned an entire generation of American jewelers into rock hounds. Three of the best were the Marcus family, Theodore B. Starr, and Louis Comfort Tiffany. They all showed exceptional design flair when they worked with unusual semiprecious gems.

Marcus advertisement from the mid-twenties written and illustrated by Rockwell Kent.

MARCUS

Rockwell Kent, a graphic artist who was famous for the best-selling novels he wrote and illustrated about his travels in the wilderness, did the advertising campaign for the American jeweler Marcus in the twenties. Kent's ads had bold atmospheric illustrations and adventurous text that described the history of gems and depicted the Marcus family as heroes in the esoteric art of finding them. One ad called "Filling the Treasure Chest," read, "In European markets where jewelers gather, the principals of the firm of Marcus & Company are familiar figures. Personally, they fill anew each season the treasure chests of this establishment. They buy frequently, largely and for cash."

The gem-buying legend immortalized by Kent began in 1892 with the father and son partnership of Herman and William

Marcus. George Elder (1859–1917), Herman's second son, joined the team around the turn of the century. The family's eye for stones went beyond fabulous precious gems to unusual semiprecious varieties, a topic William Marcus believed in passionately. During the 1880s,William co-authored a small book with his former partner George Jacques called *Something About Neglected Gems,* written in the style of Kunz. The dazzling shapes and sophisticated color schemes of semiprecious stones, as well as unusual pearls, such as pink conch and white blister, played a part in many of the firm's interesting jewelry designs.

Black opals from Lightning Ridge, Australia, appeared in Marcus jewelry again and again. A distractingly beautiful gem and one of the most difficult to use in a design—most jewelers set opals in plain mounts with little embellishment—the movement of the blues, greens, oranges, and pinks in the stone itself provided a lot of excitement. Marcus added a level of complexity to this

Details of a Gothic cathedral are deftly recreated in a little gold and opal brooch made by Marcus during the early years of the twentieth century. Light and dark blue black opals, set in a lozenge pattern, recreate the look of traditional marble floors in old churches.

A brooch made by Marcus in the early years of the twentieth century features a carved black opal cameo of Aurora, goddess of the dawn, flying through a sky lit up by diamonds. Demantoid garnet fish and seaweed decorate the bottom of the ocean.

already complex stone. One brooch had a diamond Spanish galleon speeding over a black opal sea under a white opal sky. Another brooch featured a pattern of light and black opals within the outline of a gold Gothic cathedral. A third brooch contained a carved black opal cameo of Aurora, the Greek goddess of the dawn, floating over the ocean.

Throughout the twenties and thirties Marcus was a top firm in New York and Palm Beach with offices in Paris and Bombay. Superior salesmen behind the counter, including Raymond C. Yard, helped to maintain its popularity. The firm went out of business in the early 1940s.

DATES: Marcus was established in 1892. The company went out of business around the time of World War II.
FOUNDER: Herman Marcus (1828–1899) and William Marcus
LOCATIONS: New York, Palm Beach

THEODORE B. STARR

In 1893 French jewelry critic Henri Vever went to Chicago to cover the World's Fair. On his way back to Paris, he stopped off in New York to check out a few jewelers, among them Theodore B. Starr. One of the biggest firms in the city, T. B. Starr took up almost an entire city block, from 206 Fifth Avenue to 1126 Broadway. Back in Paris, Vever wrote in an article titled "Rapport" that the firm's work was interesting and even remarkable.

The founder, Theodore B. Starr, had worked his way up from the bottom of the jewelry industry, beginning as an office boy at Reed, Taylor & Co. in 1853. Nine years later, Starr started a small commission business, which he named Starr & Marcus when Herman Marcus joined him as a partner. In 1877 Starr bought out Marcus' share and moved into his colossal quarters on Fifth Avenue. The inventory included everything from trinkets to silver trophies, but it was his jewelry, more than anything else, that made Starr special.

One of the few extant T. B. Starr jewels, a Celtic-style brooch, reveals Mr. Starr's superior eye for gems and his interest in the arts—he had been a lifetime member of the Metropolitan Museum of Art. The piece was inspired by the textured, interlocking, snake-like coils of Irish goldwork from around the twelfth century. The sharply defined surface patterns of pellets, braids, and crimped wire reveal that Starr and his designers were, without a doubt, spending time in libraries and museums studying the art of the past. The Mexican fire opal was a modern-day embellishment at the center of the design. Its orangish flame lit up the jewel.

When Theodore B. Starr died in 1907, his two sons, Louis and Howard, took over the firm. In 1912 they moved to the new center of luxury trade in New York on Fifth Avenue and Forty-seventh Street. For its fiftieth anniversary, the firm published an 1862 letter in *Vogue* signed by eight prominent jewelers attesting to Mr. Starr's integrity, faithfulness, and business experience. T. B. Starr was sold to Reed & Barton Corporation at the end of World War I and closed in 1923.

DATES: 1862–1923
FOUNDER: Theodore B. Starr (1837–1907)
BRANCH: New York

A Mexican fire opal is the centerpiece of a Celtic-style gold brooch with diamond and sapphire accents by Theodore B. Starr.

LOUIS COMFORT TIFFANY

Charles Lewis Tiffany's son, Louis Comfort Tiffany, already had made his name in several areas of the decorative arts before he turned to jewelry. He was world famous for his multicolor stained-glass lamps featuring dragonflies and flowers. He was the number-one interior decorator on the East Coast, with the houses of Mark Twain and art collector Henry O. Havemeyer to his credit. Tiffany's line of favrile glass vases and stemware made him a star at international exhibitions.

Even though Louis Comfort had been a director of the family firm and had done small projects with the company since around 1894, he chose to sell his work through fine department stores and galleries such as Neiman Marcus in Dallas, Shreve and Company in San Francisco, Marshall Fields in Chicago, and the prestigious Samuel S. Bing L'Art Nouveau Gallery in Paris. When his father died in 1902, he became a vice-president of Tiffany & Co. He moved his glassware and lamps into the store and listed them in the firm's famous mail-order catalogue. That same year he began his experimenting in jewelry.

Louis Comfort took two years to design his first collection at his studio, Tiffany Furnaces, in New York City. Feeling the pressure of being the son of the founder of one of America's greatest jewelry firms, Louis Comfort made sure his designs were great before he showed them publicly. He asked his craftsman not to talk about his designs to anybody, and he had his assistant, Julia Munson, secretly buy exotic and unusual semiprecious gems. Louis Comfort was fascinated by semiprecious gems and often consulted with George Kunz, Tiffany & Co.'s eminent gemologist.

At the 1904 St. Louis Exposition Louis Comfort debuted twenty-seven jewels featuring nature-theme designs and semiprecious stones. A demantoid garnet and white enamel Queen Anne's Lace hair ornament and a Deadly Night Shade silver belt with clusters of Mexican fire opals, carnelians, and enameled silver bead berries excited the critics.

The Craftsman magazine effused, "To describe the beauty of these pieces is quite impossible. Even a picture of them gives but a poor idea of their effect, which results from color arrangements of natural stones and enamels employed in the most skillful and varied combinations." Similar reviews, some with exactly the same descriptions and references to historic designs, appeared in *The Jewelers Circular Weekly*, *Vogue*, and *Town & Country*, leading one of Louis Comfort Tiffany's many biographers, Janet Zapata, to the conclusion that the magazines had copied the artist's, or his publicity department's, press release verbatim. Even though Louis Comfort's jewelry for the exposition didn't have any official connection to Tiffany & Co., the power of the jewelry firm as a big advertiser in several of the magazines may have swayed editors to give the jewelry coverage in exactly the way the press releases outlined. Whatever the case may have been, the jewelry deserved a positive reception.

One piece that Louis Comfort designed around the time of the St. Louis Exposition, a magical hair comb of dragonflies and dandelions, illustrates what a gifted jewelry designer he was. A simple scene of spring, it is a complicated combination of gems and materials. Lines of opals shimmer along the back of two fully three-dimensional dragonflies with pink opal eyes. Their wings are a gossamer network of platinum attached to a cluster of twinkling

Louis Comfort Tiffany designed a flying staircase for the picture gallery of Henry O. Havemeyer's New York City home in 1892.

green demantoid garnets set in gold. The insects are gently touching down on the balls of feathery dandelion seeds made with platinum filaments and white enamel heads. The reality of the scene is enhanced by missing seeds on one of the puff balls—it looks as though they have been blown away in the wind.

In 1907 jewelry by Louis Comfort made its debut on the Tiffany & Co. selling floor. It appeared in the Blue Book under the heading "Tiffany Art Jewelry." There wasn't a special signature attached to Louis Comfort's line. Designs are attributed to him

A hair ornament by Louis Comfort Tiffany features dragonflies with black and pink opal and demantoid garnet bodies, and platinum wire wings. The platinum dandelion pods the insects have landed on have white enamel seeds and a few green and yellow enamel leaves.

on the basis of his archives, including scrapbooks, lists, a small reference library, photos, and drawings, as well as some educated guesses based on his attributed jewels.

When styles began to change from fluid and nature-theme accessories to geometric and machine-inspired jewels around the end of World War I, Louis Comfort stopped designing. In 1918 he resigned as artistic director of the firm, but remained on the board of directors. The department he formed continued to manufacture his designs under the direction of Meta Overbeck until 1933 when Louis Comfort Tiffany died.

DESIGNER: Louis Comfort Tiffany (1848–1933)
SELECT BOOKS: McKean, Hugh F. *The "Lost" Treasures of Louis Comfort Tiffany*. New York: Doubleday & Co., Inc., 1980; Zapata, Janet. *The Jewelry and Enamels of Louis Comfort Tiffany*. New York: Harry N. Abrams, 1993.
EXHIBITION: 1998, New York. *Louis Comfort Tiffany at the Metropolitan Museum of Art.*
LOCATIONS: Louis Comfort Tiffany began designing jewelry at Tiffany Furnaces around 1902. From 1907 to 1933, the jewelry was sold at Tiffany & Co. stores.

Lapis lazuli, amethyst, and brown jade are the center stones of enamel and gold brooches by Louis Comfort Tiffany.

THE MODERNISTS

At the 1925 Exposition des Arts Décoratifs et Industriels Modernes, an important art and design event with an influential panel of jurors, jewelers split into two camps, divided over the interpretation of what modern jewelry was. On the right, there was deluxe Art Deco jewelry, represented by big-name firms like Cartier, Van Cleef & Arpels, and Boucheron. These rue de la Paix and Place Vendome establishments showed bandeaux, tiaras that wrapped around the forehead, lavalieres, long necklaces with huge gem pendants, and gem-encrusted geometric wide bracelets, jewels that were just right for the upper crust of society. Flowers featured prominently in many designs. Islamic, Egyptian, and Chinese themes added spice to high-end Deco and reflected the clients' taste for travel. The new designs sent *haute joaillerie* in a new direction.

On the left, the revolutionary side, jewelers defined modernity quite differently. The leaders in this category, Georges and Jean Fouquet and Gérard Sandoz, revealed innovative design ideas they would take to the limit. While all of them came from *haute joaillerie* backgrounds, Sandoz and the Fouquets were not interested in simply dreaming up new looks for the well-to-do. These jewelers thought it was definitively modern to make designs with nonprecious materials, such as wood, string, and rock crystal. They hoped that less expensive materials would make their jewels accessible to a broader audience.

To further the public's appreciation of their avant-garde work, the Fouquets and Sandoz wrote articles and books on jewelry. Georges Fouquet's book *La Bijouterie, la Joaillerie, la Bijouterie fantaisie au XXc Siècle* was almost militant in its defense of their designs, "The ones most likely to endure are not the ostentatious displays, but those in which the metal is associated with raw materials of a financial value less than their beauty, like aquamarine, amethyst, topaz, or tourmaline. Art, which never ages, will prolong the career of these jewels. It will endow them with their true character. They will never be disassembled so that the materials can be used in a different form. They are, first of all, works of art rather than financial investments."

It was their art over commerce attitude that made these jewelers on the left, so to speak, special. They identified more closely with artists and architects than the jewelry industry. To show their allegiance to new trends, they all joined the Union des Artistes Modernes, a group of professionals committed to promoting modern art. The modernist jewelers believed art was an integral part of daily life. Modern art was in its infancy and they joined its crusade. Ultimately, however, the modernists' designs were just too edgy for the masses—all their businesses failed with the economic distress of the 1930s.

FOUQUET

Georges Fouquet was instrumental in shaping the Art Deco jewelry style. As president of the jewelry group at the 1925 Exposition des Arts Décoratifs et Industriels Modernes, he worked behind the scenes prodding his colleagues to do something new and different. To inform the public of changes taking place, he wrote extensively about modern jewelry. He steered the selection committee to choose jewelers with a vision and he hand-picked an architect to design a striking pavilion for their work. To make sure his own firm's presentation was on the cutting edge, Georges enlisted his twenty-six-year-old son, Jean, to join the group of artists contributing jewels to the Fouquet display.

Jean Fouquet (1899–1994) was at the center of the modernist movement in Paris at the time of the 1925 Exposition. He was friends with Surrealist poets Louis Aragon and Paul Eluard and was a founding member of the Union des Artistes Modernes. He had also worked on Corbusier's journal *L'Esprit Nouveau*. When Jean joined his father's firm, he became a leading jewelry designer and critic in the Art Deco movement. His key ideas appeared in his 1931 book *Jewelry and Gold*, in which he wrote, "Jewelry and gold pieces must be works of art while also responding to the same needs as industrial objects." On style, Fouquet proclaimed, "A piece of jewelry must be composed of parts that can be understood from a distance, miniatures are detestable." The strong positions young Fouquet took in his book came through in his own jewelry and in the jewelry of other designers at the firm.

African art and modern technology, the ying and yang of contemporary culture in the post World War I era, are masterfully mixed in Jean Fouquet's ebony and chrome collection. For one necklace Fouquet replicated a common African torque in a smooth

French film star Arletty poses in a silver cuff with a large semiprecious cabochon by Jean Fouquet.

Le Corbusier (left) with
Jean Fouquet in 1928.

The Depression of the 1930s hit the Fouquets hard. They had trouble getting manufacturers to produce their work, presumably because they were not paying their bills promptly. In 1936 the boutique on rue Royale closed, but that did not stop Georges and Jean from continuing their crusade to make modern jewelry. Both created designs for enthusiastic clients. In addition, Georges compiled the firm's archives as a record of jewelry history stretching from the nineteenth to the twentieth century. The Fouquet's drawings and jewelry went to the Musée des Arts Décoratifs, and the facade and interior of the Art Nouveau store,

When shipping heiress Nancy Cunard piled on bangles from Africa for a sitting with Man Ray in 1926, she ignited a trend for the bracelets.

round piece of ebony, a dark exotic wood. He added four disks, typical African jewelry motifs that didn't look so typical on this jewel because he made them in shiny chrome. The clasp and hinge, mechanisms that made it possible to open the torque and put it on, were deftly incorporated into the design as riveted chrome bands. Chrome-accented bangles were part of the bold ebony series. The bracelets were a riff on the African bangles popularized by socialite Nancy Cunard.

Jewelry created under Georges Fouquet's direction was as avant-garde as his son's, though there were differences between the two. Georges' work was inspired by the worlds of fashion and jewelry rather than contemporary art. He tweaked well-known designs such as the ubiquitous seed pearl tassel necklace popular among rue de la Paix jewelers. Fouquet took the accessory and did it his way, with frosted rock crystal beads for the necklace, a piece of black onyx with red lacquer bands for a suspension ring, and a bunch of nylon strings with crystal and onyx beads dangling under a carved crystal dome. The tassel shows the mind of a revolutionary jeweler at work. It's as if he were saying, if you must have a tassel necklace to be chic—and, during the Art Deco period, many women thought they did—choose one that is original.

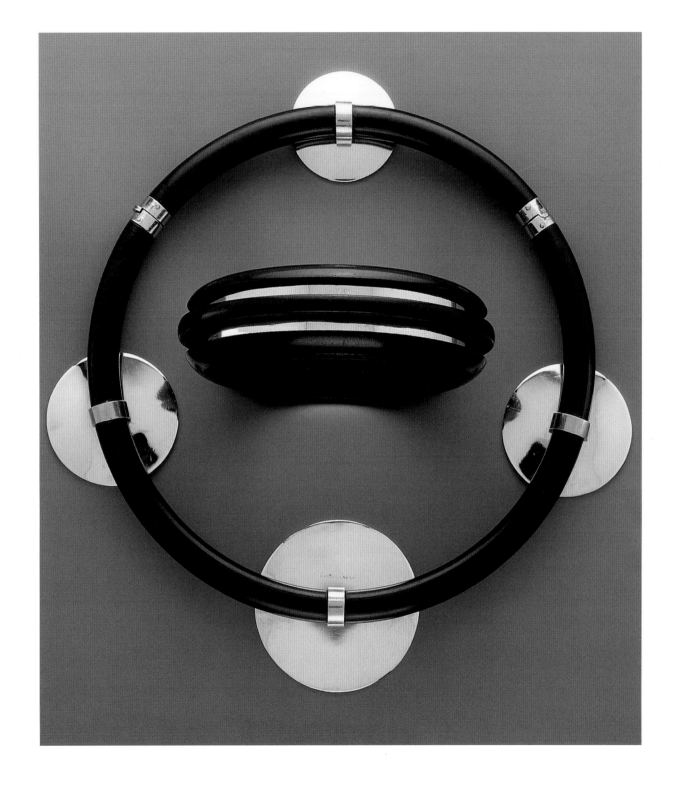

Jean Fouquet mixed ebony, chrome, and gold in a necklace and bangle made around 1931.

which had been dismantled in 1923 to make way for Art Deco, were donated to the Musée Carnavalet. Jean remained in demand as a distinguished lecturer in the field and displayed his designs at important art and jewelry shows until about 1960.

DATES: 1862–1936
FOUNDER: Alphonse Fouquet (1828–1911)
LOCATION: Paris
BOOK: *Les Fouquet. Exhibition catalogue.* Paris: Musée des Art Décoratifs, 1983.
EXHIBITION: 1983, Paris. *Les Fouquet.* Musée des Art Décoratifs, Zurich Museum Bellerive.

A frosted rock crystal pendant decorated with a collage of semiprecious stones by Jean Fouquet.

A tassel necklace by Georges Fouquet made of frosted rock crystal, nylon string, and onyx with lipstick-red enamel highlights.

GÉRARD SANDOZ

When Gérard Sandoz threw a reception at his boutique in 1928, the party was well covered by the media and attended by the crème de la crème of the Paris avant-garde. Architects, painters, editors, and interior decorators flocked to 10 rue Royale to get a look. A star of the Art Deco era, Sandoz's work also attracted tourists who went to the boutique to gawk at the unusual jewelry. As a guidebook for Americans in Paris put it, Sandoz was "the most modern of moderns."

The son of a jeweler, Sandoz followed his father on the path of modernism. The senior Sandoz, Gustave-Roger, had built the firm's reputation for modernism at the style-conscious 1900 Paris Exposition. A member of the jewelry jury, he played an active part in the Art Nouveau movement. He also had a hand in the start of Art Deco. Georges Fouquet cited him as the man who had the idea "to renovate applied decorative art by means of an international competition" in the introduction to the catalogue of the 1925 Exposition, *Le Grand Negoce: Organe du commerce de luxe française.*

In the jazz age, Gérard Sandoz cranked the firm's reputation for modernism up a notch by creating vanguard designs and writing highly intellectual, sometimes ponderous, articles on the subject. In his 1929 piece, "The Renaissance of French Art," Sandoz wrote, "It is necessary to put everything back into its rightful place, exactly as it was originally, and not to assume a belief that art is necessarily everywhere or nowhere, but to know that it is often there simply, and very naturally, without it always being necessary to add a décor." His conclusion went right to the point: "A piece of jewelry must be simple, clear, and be made without any unnecessary embellishments."

True to his word, Sandoz made jewelry that was clear, although its simplicity was debatable. Slabs of semiprecious stones and gold caused the jewelry to appear simple from a distance: close-up was another matter. Different colors of gold—red, white, yellow, and pink—gave Sandoz's designs subtle tonal effects. Gems like hematite, labradorite, and agate with off-beat shades and surfaces created a sculptural and painterly feeling. Sandoz's Guitar pendant shows off his design canon. The guitar's shapely form is composed of ridged pink gold, delicately contrasted by two white gold geometric bails.

Columnar pieces of marble-like agate and frosted crystal, outlined in black enamel, slice through the center of the pendant. Decidedly artistic, the pendant could be defined as Cubist, with various materials thrown together like a collage: a guitar motif with the muted hues of yellowed newspapers.

In 1931 the Depression caught up with Sandoz, who had always charged for his ideas rather than for the intrinsic value of materials. He was forced to close the family boutique and sold his inventory to his manufacturer, Lenfant. A multitalented artist, Sandoz retired from jewelry at age twenty-nine and became a painter, among other creative pursuits.

DATES: 1865–1931
FOUNDER: Gustave Sandoz (1836–1891)
LOCATION: Paris

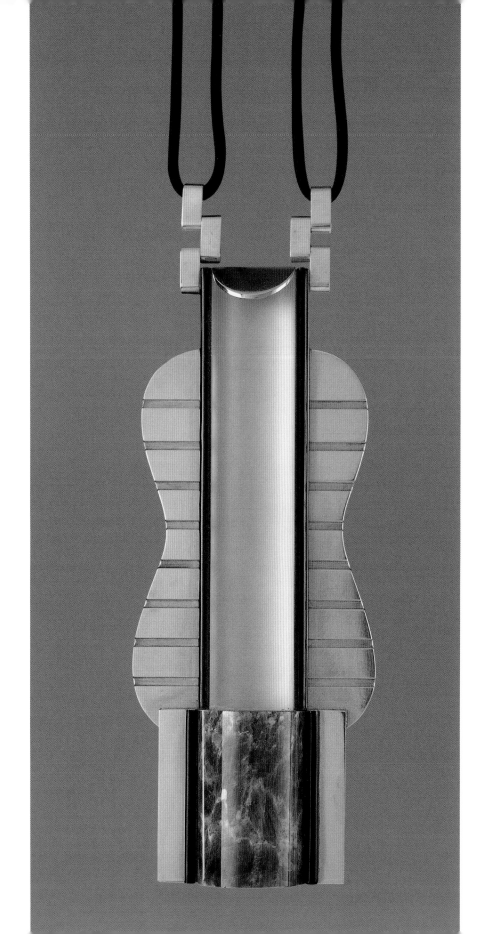

A piece of frosted crystal is at the center of Gérard Sandoz's labradorite, lacquer, pink and white gold Guitar pendant. The jewel is suspended from a black silk cord necklace.

AMERICAN STYLE

At its best, American style is sleek, sporty, and modern. It is subtle without flashy details. The look is understated, yet there is an element of luxury. In terms of clothing, this translates into the classic cashmere twin set. In jewelry, it translates into the perfectly matched string of pearls that is frequently a part of wealthy American women's jewelry boxes. In 1929 John D. Rockefeller bought his wife, Abby Aldrich, a necklace of natural rose-colored pearls from Raymond C. Yard. It had taken the jeweler ten years to find enough pearls in the right color and size for the 16-inch strand. This exceptional necklace had something in common with all good strands of pearls: it was an extravagantly expensive piece of jewelry that whispers, rather than shouts, wealth.

A simple ring with a flawless precious gem is another purely American look—a no frills way to display the perfect diamond, emerald, ruby, or sapphire. It was Charles Lewis Tiffany, after all, who invented a pretty but plain prong setting in 1886 made to show off a single diamond's brilliance. American women applauded what the setting did for their stones and they went to Tiffany in droves, turning the design into a perennial bestseller. Tiffany's biggest competitor in the early part of the century, Black, Starr & Frost, made a regular practice of mounting large gems in simple settings long before Harry Winston became known for doing big gems American-style. In the late twenties, Black, Starr & Frost mounted the 127-carat Portuguese diamond as the centerpiece on a basic choker of baguette-cut diamonds for socialite Peggy Hopkins Joyce.

Only a handful of American jewelers have done expensive simplicity to perfection. A list of the best includes two big names, Tiffany and Harry Winston, as well as Bailey, Banks & Biddle, Greenleaf & Crosby, Shreve & Co., Shreve, Crump and Low, J. E. Caldwell, Raymond C. Yard, and several that have gone out of business, among them, Udall & Ballou, Marcus, and Charlton.

When these jewelers created designs that strayed from the American credo, they were usually looking to Paris for ideas. Americans followed European jewelry trends faithfully from the beginning of the twentieth century to the end. Standard European historical motifs like Greek temples, Viking sailing ships, and Celtic knots turned up in American jewelry. Only a few jewelers gave the gemmy treatment to American life. Raymond C. Yard and Charlton were two who added jewelry with American themes to their high-end repertoire.

CHARLTON & CO.

One of the best jewelers in America during the 1920s, Charlton & Co. had been virtually unknown to the world at large until Edward, the Prince of Wales, bought a yellow and rose gold cigarette case in two engine-turned patterns. The news of his purchase during his trip to America hit the press, inspiring a barrage of lookalike Prince of Wales cigarette cases. What attracted the best-dressed man in Europe to a small, upstairs American jeweler was the firm's reputation for great designs which had spread by word of mouth across the Atlantic.

Charlton began to Charleston, so to speak, in 1919 on the eve of the roaring twenties when Grant A. Peacock and James Todd purchased founder John W. Charlton's shares and joined Robert S. Chapin, an original partner. One of the firm's greatest assets was the French designer Maurice Duvalet, who spent a certain amount of time every year trend watching in Paris. Back in New York Duvalet Americanized the French Art Deco look so deftly that the partners had no problems selling the jewels from Charlton boutiques in New York and Palm Beach without ever advertising.

Duvalet specialized in sleek long earrings, tassel necklaces, and twenty-four- to thirty-six-inch necklaces with donut-shaped crystals. These jewels could be worn frequently, and with many different gowns. The designs were not an artistic risk. They were right for Americans who simply wanted to be current.

During the slowdown of the Depression years, Duvalet kept busy by drawing caricatures of clients who dropped by the boutique, and taking on special commissions of jewels and objects. One of his most amazing special commissions was a "six-panel safari bracelet with a diamond tiger, water buffalo, rhinoceros, lion, antelope, and ram against a black lacquer and gold wilderness background. This semiformal jewel showed the Americans' attraction to the call of the wild. Hemingwayesque in their leisure pursuits, the same couple also commissioned a cigarette box to celebrate deep sea fishing in the Florida keys.

A diamond Art
Deco necklace by
Charlton displays
a donut-shape
crystal.

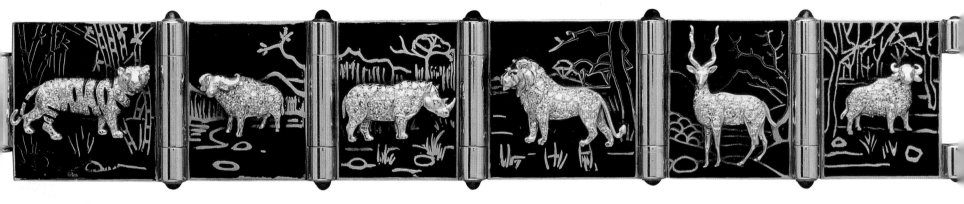

A safari bracelet and deep-sea fishing cigarette case, made by Charlton in 1937, have diamond animals and fish with enamel details and ruby and sapphire eyes in black lacquer and gold landscapes.

The box shows a dream catch of six huge diamond fish set against black enamel and gold palm trees.

Even though special commissions were made through the Depression, Charlton was debilitated by the hard times. At the outbreak of World War II, the firm had to give up its workshop and let Duvalet go. He went to work for John Rubel Co., a French manufacturer based in New York, and then to Van Cleef & Arpels, where he finished his career making magnificent designs like Jules Bache's Red Boy brooch. When Todd died in 1943, Chapin and Peacock liquidated the assets of Charlton: Chapin retired, and Grant Peacock and his son formed Grant A. Peacock, Inc.

DATES: 1909–1943
FOUNDER: John W. Charlton
LOCATIONS: New York, Palm Beach, and Paris

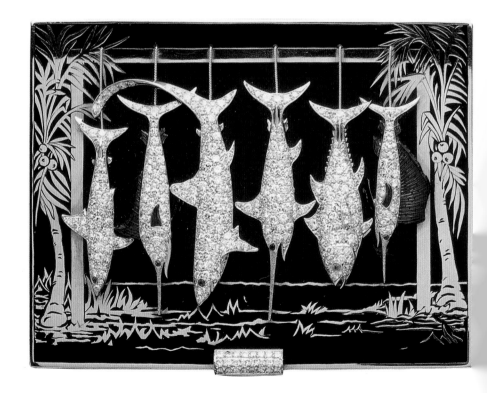

RAYMOND C. YARD

John D. Rockefeller did a big favor for Raymond C. Yard his jewelry salesman at Marcus, in the early years of the century. The millionaire told Yard if he started his own business, he would buy most of his jewelry from him and tell his friends and family to do the same. This promise enabled Yard to open the doors of his New York City boutique in 1922 with a top-drawer client list.

The sterling qualities which had impressed Rockefeller—integrity, discretion, and a thorough knowledge of jewelry—quickly made the young proprietor a confidant of protocol-conscious Americans ready to spend large sums on his firm's crisp and clean-lined Art Deco jewelry. Yard's conservative clientele also appreciated the service and location of his upstairs boutique which was removed from the hustle and bustle of street-level shops. The exclusivity and by-appointment-only rule showed Yard's understanding of his clients' lifestyle. He knew all about etiquette and formality and he also knew about the favorite leisure activities and the lighter side of well-to-do living.

A series of bunny brooches, created from the twenties through the fifties, were fun examples of the firm's work. During Prohibition, when people were forced to have cocktail hour illegally in speakeasies, Yard made bunny waiter brooches carrying trays of drinks. These little protest statements were impeccably designed and manufactured. One rabbit wore ruby pants and a diamond jacket with specially cut emeralds along the lapel and cuffs. Tiny flourishes on the piece extended to the specially cut sapphires trimming the diamond napkin, the triangle-shape diamonds forming champagne glasses, and the cube-shaped diamond ice filling the champagne bucket. Other bunny brooches made over the years included a ship captain and a bride.

Yard's coziness with his clients led to little house brooches that were replicas of their homes. In the postwar era, the house commissions reflected the prosperity of the country. A huge California modern mansion was miniaturized into a gemmy brooch with the American flag flying in the front yard. George Flagler Matthews had his East Coast home and swimming pool in Rye, New York, rebuilt as a pin in precious gems for his wife, Jean. Other brooches were more along the lines of the American dream house with a white picket fence. Yard relandscaped these

Mrs. John D. Rockefeller's natural rose-color pearl necklace by Raymond C. Yard features a marquise diamond and platinum clasp.

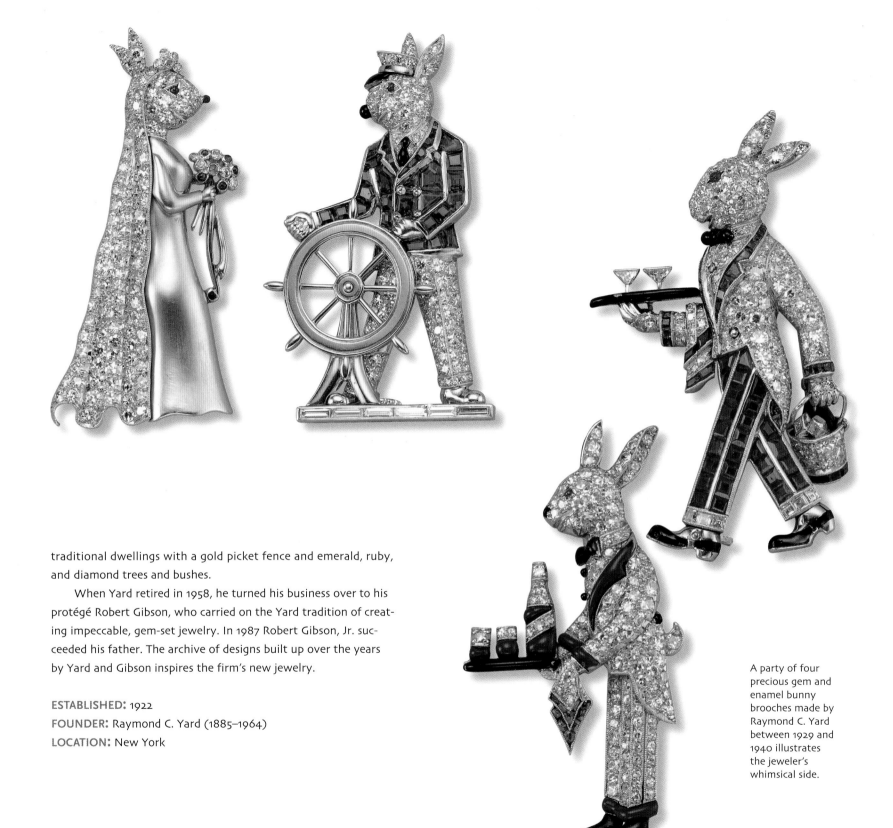

traditional dwellings with a gold picket fence and emerald, ruby, and diamond trees and bushes.

When Yard retired in 1958, he turned his business over to his protégé Robert Gibson, who carried on the Yard tradition of creating impeccable, gem-set jewelry. In 1987 Robert Gibson, Jr. succeeded his father. The archive of designs built up over the years by Yard and Gibson inspires the firm's new jewelry.

ESTABLISHED: 1922
FOUNDER: Raymond C. Yard (1885–1964)
LOCATION: New York

A party of four precious gem and enamel bunny brooches made by Raymond C. Yard between 1929 and 1940 illustrates the jeweler's whimsical side.

A diamond house
brooch, built by
Raymond C. Yard in
1961, flaunts a gold
roof and a ruby
chimney. On the
green enamel lawn
are carved emerald
shrubs, a tree with
ruby, diamond, and
emerald leaves, and
a gold picket fence.

HOLLYWOOD INSIDERS

In the midst of the financial crisis of the Depression, the public liked all their Hollywood heroines, whether they were con artists or debutantes, dressed to the nines. Actresses were under long-term contracts to the studios, and the studios made sure their marquee names looked impeccable. Hairdressers, makeup artists, and costume designers worked around the clock to fine-tune the look of actresses, on screen and off.

Jewelry played more than just a bit part in the creation of a star's image. Leading ladies flaunted gemmy treasures in publicity photos and at movie premieres and nightclubs. On the silver screen jewelers who loaned accessories to the stars were listed in the credits. During this high-glamour moment, two very different jewelers, Paul Flato and Trabert & Hoeffer-Mauboussin, became local favorites of the celebrity A-list. Describing their styles in terms of Hollywood movie genres, Flato was a screwball comedy while Trabert & Hoeffer-Mauboussin came off as a melodrama.

At a 1940 party Flato and dancer Irene Castle examine an acorn necklace and bracelet made of light to dark topaz.

FLATO

In the thirties, Paul Flato was to jewelry what Cole Porter was to movie scores. Accessories by Flato were elegant, sophisticated and funny, or as Porter might have said, de-regal, de-royal, de-Ritz, and de-lovely. Even the award-winning advertising campaign Flato wrote himself was positively Porteresque with its screwball patter of dialogue. One ad poked fun at the competitiveness of Flato clients: "It is indeed gratifying to have your dearest friend *or* fondest enemy rush up, exclaiming, 'Darling! Where did you get that *perfectly marvelous, amazing* new clip?' And it is even more gratifying to be able to answer, 'Oh, my dear, it's one of Paul Flato's new designs!'"

Paul Flato, whose approach to jewelry could be described as "Anything Goes," was the creative dynamo behind his firm, although he never actually put pen to paper. "I don't know how to draw a line. I am a creator of jewels and guide my designers," he once said. Adolph Kleaty, the firm's head designer, was the one who carried out most of his brainstorms, such as the diamond and platinum ring Katharine Hepburn wore in *Holiday (1938)*, which was inspired by a dancing girl's toe ring Flato bought in Egypt.

Flato's irreverence in jewelry probably stemmed from the fact that he didn't carry the baggage of an East Coast background. Like Cole Porter, Flato came from a small town in the sticks. He was born in Shiner, Texas. In this unlikely place he discovered his calling. "My first love of jewels," Flato confessed, "came from watching the gypsies who camped near us in Texas tinkering and making jewels—never dreaming I too would be a tinker one day. I was ten years old and would watch for hours." By 1928, at twenty-eight years old, Flato was a New Yorker with an upstairs jewelry salon at one East 57th Street, making whoopee in jewelry for East Coast dynasties and entrepreneurs who had sold short on Wall Street.

Ten years later Flato found his spiritual home in Los Angeles. His friends, silent-screen stars Constance Collier and Charlie Chaplin, scouted a location at 8637 Sunset Boulevard, just across from the Trocadero night club. The party of three celebrated the branch opening with a mob of notables including Douglas Fairbanks, Ziegfeld comedienne Fanny Brice, *Gentleman Prefer Blondes* author Anita Loos, and Twentieth Century-Fox production chief Darryl F. Zanuck. Paris couturier Elsa Schiaparelli flew in for the bash.

Charlie Chaplin dances with his wife, the actress Paulette Goddard, who is decked out in a Flato wrap-around diamond feather necklace.

A ruby and diamond three-part Flato brooch designed by Verdura was Joan Crawford's lavish accessory at an elegant 1938 movie premiere.

Marlene Dietrich was extravagantly glamorous in her emerald and diamond brooch and two bracelets by Trabert & Hoeffer-Mauboussin at a movie premiere she attended with Douglas Fairbanks in the mid-1930s.

In the screwball comedy *Holiday* (1938), Katharine Hepburn sparkled in a triple-strand diamond necklace, a yellow diamond sunburst brooch, and a charming diamond toe-ring. All of the star's jewelry in the movie was by Paul Flato.

The star attraction for these celebrities was Flato's formal jewelry. Every gemmy Flato jewel was a unique performance with an unexpected twist. A rose was never just a rose bracelet at Flato. It was a rambler that twined around the wrist on a baguette-cut diamond stem sprouting rose-cut diamond buds. Flato transformed a large quill with unruly wisps into a light-as-a-feather diamond and platinum necklace for Paulette Goddard. Cole Porter, who not surprisingly was a Flato fan, buckled-up his wife, Linda, in a calibre-cut aquamarine and ruby belt necklace.

Other attractions at Flato's boutique came from his part-time design team that was one of the most unorthodox ever assembled. When Josephine Forrestal, wife of FDR's Secretary of the Navy, blew into Flato's salon one day with some rough sketches, he liked them so much he said, "Won't you sit down and stay?" Though she was no nine-to-fiver, the socialite came up with some imaginative ideas. French crown jewels set *en tremblant* inspired

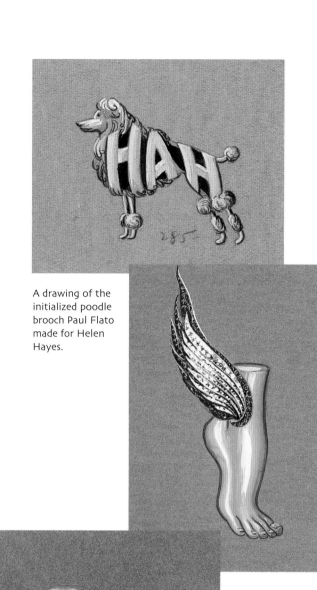

A drawing of the initialized poodle brooch Paul Flato made for Helen Hayes.

At a 1939 party at the Flato salon, Fanny Brice, Virginia Zanuck, and Reginald Gardiner admire a jewel held by Constance Collier.

A couple of whimsical designs from Paul Flato.

A niece of screenwriter Anita Loos, Mary Anita Loos shows her jewel to Charlie Chaplin at the opening party of the Flato shop in Los Angeles.

Cole Porter's wife, Linda, buckled-up in this calibre-cut aquamarine and ruby necklace by Flato.

her "wiggly" clips. She translated Victorian furniture into tufted gold boxes with diamond buttons. When Forrestal brought her friend Millicent Rogers to work one day, the Standard Oil heiress lingered just long enough to dream up "puffy" hearts, a design Flato improvised into brooches and earrings. Fashion editor Diana Vreeland introduced Fulco, Duke of Verdura, to Flato. The Duke's designs at Flato included things like Joan Crawford's three-part diamond and ruby rococo clip from pieces of stucco scrolls, which evoked his youth in a palazzo in Sicily.

Flato's clever daytime jewels broadcast his wit all over Hollywood and kept his clients coming back for more and more. The pieces also revealed little details about the stars' character or hobbies. Irene Castle slipped on a pair of gold feet brooches with ruby toenails. The pins were a pun on her maiden name, Foote, as well as a play on her dancing. Orson Welles had his name in dramatic movie marquee lettering on a watch fob. A Greek-head brooch with diamond curls lent a classical touch to Ginger Rogers's sex appeal. Joan Bennett put her fate in a Hand of God brooch by Flato. Five diamond stars representing the gods Jupiter, Saturn, Apollo, Mercury, Mars, and the Moon twinkled around a gold hand. Animal lover Helen Hayes had her French poodle immortalized in a gold brooch with her initials on the body.

Unfortunately, Flato's heyday in Hollywood didn't last too long. He was out of business on both coasts by 1943. After being convicted of pawning consigned jewels and not paying the owners, he served sixteen months in prison, and then went to Mexico in 1945 where he lived for almost eight years fighting extradition on additional charges of grand larceny and forgery involving around $60,000 in gems. In 1953 Flato returned to the United States to settle with the law. More or less unscathed by the scandal, in 1970

Flato opened a jewelry store in Mexico City that was an attraction for locals, tourists, and his old Hollywood client list until it closed in 1990.

DATES: 1928–1943
FOUNDER: Paul Flato (1900–1999)
SOME MOVIE CREDITS: *Holiday* (1938), *Blood and Sand* (1941), *That Uncertain Feeling* (1941), *Two-Faced Woman* (1941)
LOCATIONS: New York, Los Angeles, Mexico City (1970–1990)

TRABERT & HOEFFER-MAUBOUSSIN

Bold and flashy Trabert & Hoeffer-Mauboussin jewels were perfect for melodramatic Hollywood scripts. In a scene from the *Vogues of '38,* a movie about a fashion designer's struggle to stay in business, Joan Bennett models a Trabert & Hoeffer-Mauboussin diamond panel necklace with an 83-carat cabochon ruby in a make-or-break fashion show. Needless to say, Joan Bennett's strut down the catwalk in the Trabert & Hoeffer jewel and a stunning dress saves her boyfriend's design house from bankruptcy. In *Stage Door,* Trabert & Hoeffer-Mauboussin jewels were part of the ups and downs of Eve Arden's life in the fast lane. Sassy in the beginning, the showgirl educates a rookie about the spoils of the chorus line: "That's a little thing called a star sapphire." Near the end, when she loses her man to the newcomer, Arden sniffs, "In the meantime, I have my lovely sable coat and star sapphire to keep me company."

By the time Trabert & Hoeffer-Mauboussin jewelry reached the silver screen, William Howard Hoeffer was the sole proprietor of the firm. (His co-founder R. J. Trabert had died around 1934. Mauboussin was the name of the French firm that granted Trabert & Hoeffer permission to use its name and trademark in the United States from around 1934 to 1953.) A pioneer among big name east coast jewelers, Mr. Hoeffer saw the potential of Hollywood and went west to be a part of the action. Shortly after Hoeffer opened a branch in Los Angeles around 1935 he broke into the movies with the production of the *Gilded Lily* starring Claudette Colbert. The screen credit, which was one of the first for a jeweler, read "Jewels created by William Howard Hoeffer."

Hoeffer's biggest break came when Marlene Dietrich decided to become the unofficial Trabert & Hoeffer-Mauboussin poster girl. There was a period in the thirties when Dietrich wore her Trabert & Hoeffer-Mauboussin 128-carat cabochon emerald and diamond bracelet and 97-carat cabochon emerald and diamond brooch constantly. She flaunted the set in two movies, *Desire* (1936) and *Angel* (1937). Photographs by Edward Steichen and Clarence Sinclair Bull show Dietrich using the jewels as dramatic elements. Paparazzi shots prove she also wore the emeralds out on the town.

Like art directors in the thirties movies, Trabert & Hoeffer-Mauboussin did a Hollywood version of the Art Deco style, which is to say it blew-up proportions, streamlined details, and worked in a dichromatic palette. The firm made the Art Deco wide bracelet wider, blocking out all the parts, wedges, cylinders, and knobs with pavè-set diamonds. Lines of baguettes highlighted the mechanical curves. The core of the design was always a huge cabochon.

Trabert & Hoeffer-Mauboussin cabochons dazzled in photographs and movies, where the audiences couldn't decipher the quality, which was sometimes good and other times questionable. Douglas Fairbanks gave his bride Mary Pickford a Trabert & Hoeffer diamond brooch with one of the firm's prize gems, a 182-carat star sapphire dubbed The Star of Bombay. Near the end of her life Pickford bequeathed the fine star sapphire to the National Gem Collection at the Smithsonian Institution where it is part of the permanent display. On the other hand, Marlene Dietrich's emerald and the 83-carat cabochon ruby that appeared in the *Vogues of '38* and eventually landed in the collection of skating star Sonja Henie, were more about size and flash than gemology and gem quality.

Trabert & Hoeffer-Mauboussin faded out of the Hollywood picture during World War II. When William Howard Hoeffer retired and sold the business in the fifties, the Hollywood chapter closed for good. Mauboussin took back the rights to its name around 1954. Although the firm continues to create beautiful jewelry, it has never again attained Hollywood insider status.

ESTABLISHED: around 1929
FOUNDERS: R. J. Trabert and William Howard Hoeffer
FILMS: *Desire* (1936), *Angel* (1937), *Conquest* (1937), *It's All Yours* (1937), *Stage Door* (1937), *The Vogues of '38* (1937), *The Women* (1939)
LOCATIONS: During the 1930s and 1940s, there were branches in New York, Beverly Hills, Chicago, Palm Beach, Paris, Miami Beach, and Atlantic City. A store in Chicago is the only one still open.

Ann Warner (left), wife of the studio chief Jack Warner, put on her emerald cabochon pendant necklace by Trabert & Hoeffer-Mauboussin for a night on the town in Hollywood. She is joined at her table by Errol Flynn's wife, Lili Damita, Marlene Dietrich, Jack Warner, and Errol Flynn.

Marlene Dietrich wore her Trabert & Hoeffer-Mauboussin emerald and diamond brooch, bracelet, and ring in *Desire* (1936).

Marlene Dietrich's diamond bracelet by Trabert & Hoeffer-Mauboussin features a 128-carat cabochon emerald. Her brooch has a 97-carat cabochon emerald.

THE ARTISTS

In the sixties and seventies, when it was fashionable for artists to make jewelry, several twentieth-century masters dabbled in accessory design. The most high-profile artist to turn his talents to the field was Pablo Picasso, who modeled some tiny African masks for cast gold pendants. In 1974 sculptor Louise Nevelson shrunk her monumental wood assemblages down into a series of wood and gold brooches measuring approximately 2½ inches high. Pop artist Roy Lichtenstein designed silver and enamel pendants in 1968. One piece, a female bust, titled Modern Head, showed his trademark Benday dots.

Commercialized versions of the artists' masterworks, these accessories did not add anything significant to jewelry design. Picasso's African masks lost almost all their primitivism on the way to becoming pendants. Ill-conceived benday dots in enamel gave Lichtenstein's heads a case of chicken pox. And Nevelson's brooch assemblages looked as though there had not been much assembly required.

Two artists who did contribute to the art of jewelry were Alexander Calder and Salvador Dalí. Dalí headed for the glitz and glamour of high-end jewelry, designing surreal pieces in precious gems and working with a fine jewelry manufacturer, while Calder went in the opposite direction, pounding and forging brass, silver, and gold into bracelets, pendants, and tiaras in his sculpture studio. The attention these two great artists paid to the jewelry medium fired-up fashion editors who gave their work lots of coverage. Their incredibly original designs moved jewelry forward. Calder's metal jewels introduced a whole new vocabulary of spiral motifs to studio jewelry that is still enormously influential. And Dalí's surrealist pieces, like his ruby lips, still stand out to this day as a bold, daring, and novel use of precious gems.

ALEXANDER CALDER

At mid-century women who liked off-beat accessories wore jewelry by Alexander Calder. His jewels were especially popular with the New York gallery crowd. Folk-art collector Jean Lipman shimmered

Calder works on one of his wire sculptures.

at openings in a brass and silver Calder bracelet with twelve different swirl charms. Mary Rockefeller required a little elbow room at modern art exhibits when she put on her brass Calder necklace with heart and harp motifs that flared out to her sides. Not one to be upstaged, Peggy Guggenheim, a titan among New York art collectors, commissioned a pair of 6½-inch-wide mobile earrings in silver. "Every woman in New York who is fortunate enough to be decorated by a Calder jewel has a brooch or a bracelet or a necklace," Guggenheim wrote in her autobiography *Out of this Century: Confessions of an Art Addict.* "I am the only woman in the world who wears his enormous mobile earrings."

Calder had become a darling of the art world with his imaginative sculptures. These works, a delicately balanced series of biomorphic motifs that hung from the ceiling on a single cable and moved, were dubbed "mobiles" by Marcel Duchamp. Calder's work was difficult to categorize, but art historians put

Georgia O'Keeffe wears her "OK" initial brooch by Calder sideways in 1945.

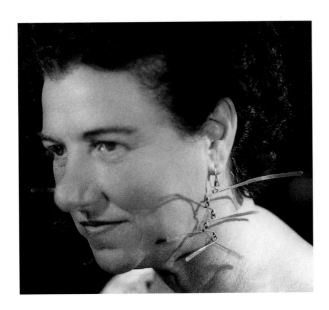

Peggy Guggenheim models
Calder mobile earrings.

English art historian Sir
Kenneth Clark bought
his wife a Calder tiara at
the Freddy Mayor
Gallery in England. The
delicate brass jewel, a
circlet with a row of
tapered spiral finials,
undoubtedly turned a
few crowned heads on
formal occasions.

Gérard Philipe embraces Jeanne Moreau wearing her Calder bracelet in a publicity still for the 1952 play *Nuclea*.

Brass and simple cord are the materials in Lady Kenneth Clark's Calder necklace.

him on a par with other highly individualistic sculptors such as Diego Giacometti and Henry Moore.

From the moment he emerged on the art scene in the late twenties, Calder made jewelry. Some of his first wire earrings, caricatures of well-known Parisian ladies, were similar to his small wire Josephine Baker sculptures. In 1931 Calder changed the look of his jewelry beginning with an engagement ring he made for his wife, Louisa. For the design he took a single piece of wire, heated it, and hammered it flat. Then he shaped it into a triple-band ring with a spiral on top. The flat metal characterized the majority of his jewels from then on, and the spiral appeared over and over in his brass, copper, silver, and gold necklaces, bracelets, brooches, rings, and at least one tiara.

Calder jewels were sold at a few different art galleries in London and at Marian Willard in New York. Another way to obtain a piece of Calder jewelry was to have a special relationship with the artist. He made numerous pieces for his many friends.

For Georgia O'Keeffe he created a clever "OK" brooch, which she wore sideways on her lapel. Jeanne Moreau wore her Calder spiral cuff on-stage and screen. The French actress even managed to squeeze a joke about the jewel into François Truffaut's 1967 film *The Bride Wore Black*. When a painter handed her the cuff to wear for a portrait, he said, "It's not junk. It's by Calder."

ARTIST: Alexander Calder (1898–1976)
SELECT BOOKS: Marchesseau, Daniel. *The Intimate World of Alexander Calder*. Exhibition catalogue. Paris: Solange Thierry Editeur, 1989; Prather, Marla with contributions by Alexander S. C. Rower and Arnauld Pierre. *Alexander Calder 1898–1976*. Exhibition catalogue. New Haven and London: Yale University Press, 1998.
A FEW OF THE EXHIBITIONS: 1998, Washington, D. C. *Alexander Calder 1898–1976*, National Gallery of Art, San Francisco Museum of Modern Art; 1989, Paris. *The Intimate World of Alexander Calder*. Musée des Arts Décoratifs, Mexico City, El Centro Cultural/Arte Contemporáneo, New York, Cooper-Hewitt Museum.
MOVIE CREDIT: *The Bride Wore Black* (1967)

SALVADOR DALÍ

Salvador Dalì gave almost as much thought to the meaning of jewelry as he did to designing it. When four of his precious jewels appeared in a 1941 *Vogue* spread, "Dalí's Dream of Jewels," notes from his sketchbooks were included as well: "The ideal Object to me is an Object that is useful for absolutely nothing; that could not be used for writing or removing superfluous hair or for telephoning; an Object which could not be placed on the mantelpiece or a Louis XIV commode; an Object which one is forced simply to wear—a Jewel." Dalí's maxims were, without a doubt, unusual for a jewelry designer, but the idea of creating with a philosophy in mind and juxtaposing miscellaneous things was very much a part of being a Surrealist.

Dalí lived the life, imbibed the spirit, and embodied the tenets of Surrealism on a grand scale. The art movement, inspired by a late 1920s series of writings by André Breton, was about penetrating dreams and the subconscious to imagery unedited by reason. In Dalí's paintings, Breton's manifestos took the form of figures and objects, like soft faces, women with open drawers for body parts, and melting watches, super-realistically rendered in barren landscapes. Titles identified, but didn't necessarily explain, the assembly of things in a painting. For example one painting with a pomegranate, two tigers, a goldfish, an elephant with an obelisk, a shotgun, and a nude reclining figure was titled, "Dream Caused By the Flight of a Bee Around a Pomegranate a Second Before Awakening."

When Dalí's lover Gala (who became his wife in 1959) encouraged him to go to America in 1934, he became a celebrity Surrealist and even landed on the cover of *Time* magazine. This trip also marks the beginning of Dalí's forays into many different fields: he did window displays at Bonwit Teller; he collaborated on clothing and costume jewelry designs with French couturier Elsa Schiaparelli; and he designed a production for the dream sequence in Alfred Hitchcock's thriller *Spellbound* (1945). Gala was also responsible for encouraging Dalí to design precious jewelry, which he began to do around 1937.

A friend of Dalì's, Caresse Crosby was so excited by his jewelry designs that she introduced him to jewelry designer Fulco di Verdura in an effort to get his work manufactured. Verdura wrote up his first surreal encounter with Dalì at the socialite's rickety

Salvador Dalí escorts his biggest jewelry client, Rebecca Harkness, to a reception.

Verdura created a gold-hammered box with an opal beetle
in 1941 as a fancy frame for an ivory miniature by Dalí.

Dalí's Etoile de Mer brooch from the Rebecca Harkness collection included a large pearl, diamonds, rubies, emeralds, and gold. The little sculpted gold butterflies designed to be worn with the starfish have sapphires, emeralds, green, blue, brown, yellow, and white diamonds.

Andy Warhol at an art reception with Rebecca Harkness, who wears the Etoile de Mer brooch by Dalí over her breast.

Dalí's 1950 design for the Etoile de Mer brooch includes a water color of the jewel and a pen and pencil sketch of a hand modeling how it might be worn.

old Virginian manor for *Harper's Bazaar* in 1941: "Back in the sitting room. It was deathly cold. Everyone had on an overcoat. I had removed mine when I first came in and by now was too numb to ask for it." And "Dalí kept saying: 'It is the atelier of Picasso,' This I have never seen; but I am told it is of the same squalor with no ashtray emptied since the Blue period."

The tale's happy ending reveals the house was an elaborate joke on Verdura, who loved the farce thoroughly and immediately agreed to collaborate on some jewels with Dalí. A few of their designs were illustrated in Verdura's story in *Harper's Bazaar*. There was a pink tourmaline and gold Palladian door brooch with a turquoise and ruby-studded pediment featuring a bust of the nymph Daphne turning into a tree. Green-gold snakes, with ruby eyes, attacking a large morganite are the theme of another brooch decorating the page. There was also a hammered gold cigarette case with an ivory miniature by Dalí of an enormous spider with a Medusa head in a barren landscape; an opal beetle lurks on the border of the box. The collection of jewels by Dalí and Verdura was exhibited at the Julien Levy Gallery in New York together with the artist's paintings in 1941.

In 1949 Dalí signed a contract, approved by Gala, to create five designs a year until 1960 with the jewelry manufacturer Alemany, which had world rights. Alemany's ability to adapt Dalí's bizarre designs showed a great rapport with the artist. A. Hyatt Mayor, curator of prints at the Metropolitan Museum of Art, made the following observation about the relationship in 1959, "Dalí's dashing, imaginative sketches are perhaps his most likable creations, but they need a practical jeweler to translate them before their effect can be translated in metal and stones. The sketches would never get off the paper without an interpretation as thorough and as skillful as that of the orchestrator of a piano score. The interpreter has the absolute power to make or break the artist's invention, so when we applaud these remarkable jewels, Alemany should also climb onto the stage to take his bow beside the brilliant star."

Dalí made several surreal trinkets with Alemany, such as gold and gem-studded telephone ear clips and cabochon ruby and emerald leaf-veined hands sculpted in gold. His best-known jewels done in this period made clever use of jewelry materials. In Dalí's Eye of Time brooch, the eyeball within the diamond eyelid is a watch. A brooch with ruby lips and white pearl teeth was the most frequently imitated of all Dalí's jewels.

Rebecca Harkness had a number of Dalí original jewels. The best in the collection was a starfish brooch referred to as the Etoile de Mer. Wildly organic, the flexible ruby and diamond arms of the brooch were long and droopy. The body was an extra-large round pearl with a totally inexplicable set of gold and green enamel branches sprouting from the left and right side. The fantasy creature is made even more surreal by a pair of butterflies that could be attached to the arms. An element of Dalí's original drawing was a melted watch in one of the arms, but this proved impossible for Alemany to convert into the brooch. Even without the watch, the jewel was amazing, and the irrepressible Mrs. Harkness, one of the great patrons of New York ballet, added to the jewel's shock when she appeared at formal affairs in full evening dress with the starfish clinging to her breast.

Critics responded warmly to Dalí's jewelry. "I believe we are seeing the birth of a Fabergé," was part of a review in *The London Times*. Dalí "rivals the craftsmanship of Renaissance jewelers and even surpasses it in extravagance of motif and mechanical contrivance," raved Henry La Farge in *Art News*. Philip C. Johnson of the Museum of Modern Art in New York said Dalí's jewels had "great historical value."

Art critics and the public had many opportunities to view Dalí's jewelry. Twenty-two of his pieces had been purchased by the Owen Cheatham Foundation in 1954. The foundation toured the collection like an art exhibit for fund-raising events. An accompanying catalogue titled *Dalí, A Study of his Art-in-Jewels* included an essay by A. Hyatt Mayor and comments and captions by Dalí who had made a 360-degree turn on the meaning of jewelry from when he began to design in the late 1930s. Dalí wrote "The jeweled pieces you find in this book were not conceived to rest soullessly in steel vaults. They were created to please the eye, uplift the spirit, stir the imagination, express convictions."

ARTIST: Salvador Dalí (1904–1989)
SELECT BOOKS: Cowles, Fleur. *The Case of Salvador Dalí*. Boston: Little, Brown and Company, 1959; *Dalí: A Study of His Art-in Jewels, The Collection of the Owen Cheatham Foundation*. Livingston, Lida, ed. Greenwich, Ct.: New York Graphic Society, 1959.

THE MAVERICKS

Women who were famous for their style, those who achieved icon status in the twentieth century, such as the Duchess of Windsor, Jackie Kennedy, and Elizabeth Taylor, didn't cause the flashbulbs to pop by blending in. They gained attention and sparked trends by putting a unique spin on what constituted a well-dressed woman. A good eye for accessories went a long way in creating a little drama. These ladies of the highest fashion knew how to work their belts, bags, shoes, scarves, and sunglasses as well as their jewelry. For evening wear, they shopped at the big names, Bulgari, Cartier, Tiffany, Van Cleef & Arpels, and Harry Winston. For daytime and exotic evening jewels, they went to Renè Boivin, Suzanne Belperron, Fulco di Verdura, Seaman Schepps, Jean Schlumberger, and David Webb. What made these jewelers the in-group was their knightlike quest for originality. Each one pushed the envelope of good taste in precious jewelry by mixing enamel, precious and semiprecious gems, blowing up proportions, and making their themes epic. Inspiration taken from the age of chivalry, the glory that was ancient Greece, and the mystery of the Orient provided these jewelers with the imagery and colors right for women on the world stage.

BOIVIN

At a time when few women worked in the jewelry industry and even fewer were decision makers, Jeanne Boivin (1871–1959) ruled the executive offices at her own firm in Paris. Presiding over design, finance, and manufacturing were responsibilities Boivin assumed when her husband, Renè Boivin, died in 1917. Maintaining the firm's independence was the first move in her long career that would make Boivin one of the best small firms in Paris from the thirties into the early forties.

From the moment Madame Boivin took the reins, she drove things forward with her definite views on design. She hated the cold geometry of Art Deco and loved the fluid lines of Art Nouveau and Mother Nature. She felt precious gems

should be used artistically, not ostentatiously. One way she did this was by creating colorful semiprecious stone pavés and boldly studding pieces with precious cabochons. Like many chief executives in jewelry, Madame Boivin didn't draw. She hired designers to carry out her vision and the designers she chose just so happened to be women. From 1921 to 1931 Suzanne Belperron worked at Boivin. Jeanne Boivin's daughter, Germaine (1898–1985) came up with concepts for jewels from 1938 to 1976. The designer who was the creator of Boivin's best pieces, Juliette Moutard (1900–1990) was at the firm from 1934 to 1970.

The audacious designs made by these women attracted celebrated and discriminating jewelry clients. During the peak of her creativity, Boivin was patronized by artists, writers, and style icons, including Pierre Bonnard, Colette, Jean Cocteau, Francis Picabia, and Marie Laurencin. Standard Oil heiress Millicent Rogers commissioned several pieces and purchased jewels off the rack, so to speak, from Boivin. A starfish brooch Boivin reproduced several times in pavé-set amethysts

Ruby cabochons accent a gold lipstick holder by Boivin.

Two gold starfish brooches by Boivin studded with rubies, amethyst, emeralds, and aquamarines.

Millicent Rogers pinned a huge Boivin starfish brooch on her columnar wool pants suit in 1945.

Daisy Fellowes paired her
Boivin pigeon-wing brooches
with a fluffy jacket and a
choker of large cabochon
sapphires (probably by Boivin)
for a highly stylized portrait
taken by Cecil Beaton in 1930.

The sapphires in Daisy Fellowes's diamond and gold pigeon-wing brooch by Boivin were specially cut to look like feathers.

BELPERRON

Suzanne Belperron was opinionated. On the subject of antique jewelry she once said, "It was all right for Aunt Agatha's neck in her day, but worthless if it does nothing for the personality of the woman who has inherited it." Madame Belperron lit into those who held conservative views on jewelry. "For too long," she told a journalist in the forties, "there has been a decidedly archaic feeling about jewelry. Originally used as adornment, jewels have become an exaggerated and flamboyant means of expressing wealth and even snobbery, instead of enhancing beauty and reflecting personality."

Belperron was a benevolent dictator when it came to her clients, insisting that all of them, from the Duchess of Windsor to Frank Sinatra, come in person to her out-of-the-way shop at 59 rue de Chateaudun in Paris. She didn't invite them to hear about their design whims. She wanted to make sure her work fit properly and looked right on them. "Long slim fingers," she said, "require one design to enhance their beauty, while babyish shaped fingers require an entirely different treatment." Belperron's final statement, which some clients surely resented, was to make no statement at all. She never signed her pieces. Belperron believed her designs alone were the signature.

Suzanne Belperron's strong will had propelled her career since its earliest days in 1921, when she started as a salesgirl at Boivin. With no previous experience in the field of jewelry, she got the job by convincing the powers that be that she understood her generation, the younger generation, and could pull in new clients. Two years later at the age of twenty-three, she became a designer, dreaming up jewelry, often in a bold Egyptian style, under the direction of Jeanne Boivin. In her ten years at the firm, she added significantly to the jeweler's trendsetting reputation and became part of the artistic jewelry and couture community in Paris. She was befriended by Schiaparelli, who recognized her talents and sent clients her way when she left Boivin to go into business with one of Boivin's suppliers, the pearl merchant Bernard Herz.

The firm B. Herz gave Belperron the freedom to design the way she wanted. Belperron let loose with a style completely

studded with cabochon rubies, or pavé-set aquamarines and emeralds, was so individualistic that it satisfied Rogers' high standards of originality.

Singer sewing machine heiress and jewelry collector extraordinaire Daisy Fellowes went to Boivin for her plucky purchase of a pair of pigeon-wing brooches. Elegant and classical, the brooches looked more like the wings on Hermes' sandals than the mottled appendage of the urban bird. Round and baguette-cut diamonds set in gold spilled over the upper wing and buff-top sapphires lined the feathers.

The jewels Jeanne Boivin designed surpassed in creativity her husband's attractive revivalist and botanical style pieces. In a way, her career had more in common with her brother's, the clothing designer Paul Poiret's, than her husband's. While René Boivin had followed the fashionable looks of the turn of the century, Madame Boivin developed a style that set trends in the 1930s.

ESTABLISHED: 1893
FOUNDER: René Boivin (1864–1917)
BOOK: Cailles, Françoise. *René Boivin Jeweller.*
London: Quartet Books, 1994.
LOCATION: Paris

The Duchess of Windsor wears her chalcedony earrings and brooch by Belperron.

The Duchess of Windsor's chalcedony, sapphire, and diamond suite by Belperron includes two bracelets, a pair of earrings, and a necklace with a large flower that could be detached and worn as a brooch.

Suzanne Belperron wears a simple suit and one of her bold brooches to the office.

A carved smoky topaz gives heft to a platinum and diamond flower brooch by Belperron.

The Duchess of Windsor owned a quintessential Belperron suite of stained blue chalcedony made around 1935. The centerpiece of the striking set was a double-strand choker of chalcedony beads. The clasp, a huge chalcedony flower with rays of diamonds set in the petals and a cluster of eight unmatched cabochon sapphires at the center, could be worn as a brooch. Belperron's leaves were made ultra-glam in a pair of earrings with a vein of diamonds and a semisurround of cabochon sapphires and round diamonds. Two matching chalcedony cuffs with square diamonds have a row of chalcedony beads topped with tiny cabochon sapphires. The look is frankly monarchical, as the design resembles a coronet, the crown worn by the Prince of Wales.

Belperron applied the same single-mindedness that characterized her design career to running the firm in the war years. Bernard Herz, a French Jew in fear of the Nazis, had put the business in her name before the Germans marched into Paris and deported him to a concentration camp, where he died. All through the occupation, Belperron had offers from many American firms, including Tiffany, to leave Paris, but she held on to the company tenaciously and after the war was able to present it intact to Bernard Herz's son, Jean. From 1945 to 1975 they ran Herz-Belperron together. In 1991 Belperron's work gained a new audience when Edward Landrigan started having the original designs manufactured again. The new Belperron jewels are sold at Landrigan's Verdura boutiques in New York and Palm Beach.

DATES: 1933–1975, reestablished in 1991.
DESIGNER: Suzanne Belperron (1900–1983) designed for B. Herz and Herz-Belperron.
LOCATION: Paris, New York (1991)

different from Boivin's, based on an outlandish combination of precious and semiprecious stones set in bulbous pieces of clear crystal, smoky topaz, agate, and chalcedony. Newspaper journalist Rosette Hargrove wrote in 1951, "Suzanne is unorthodox in her designing methods. She has been known, for instance, to sink a 15-carat marquise diamond into a scooped-out ring of rock crystal." Extraordinary as it was to the reporter, the huge domed cocktail ring, with a gem on top, was standard Belperron fare. Her work—the abstract designs and nature motifs—was all characterized by bulbous forms.

VERDURA

Fulco di Verdura was wickedly witty on the subject of other people's jewelry. The biting commentary he dished out about large gems—he called a huge solitaire diamond ring "a swimming pool" and dismissed a necklace with a gigantic sapphire as "mineralogy not jewelry"—were just the type of spicy quips

Baked enamel and gold Maltese cross
cuffs by Verdura, studded with pearls,
precious, and semiprecious stones.

Verdura shows Coco Chanel the
white enamel Maltese cross
cuff he designed for her.

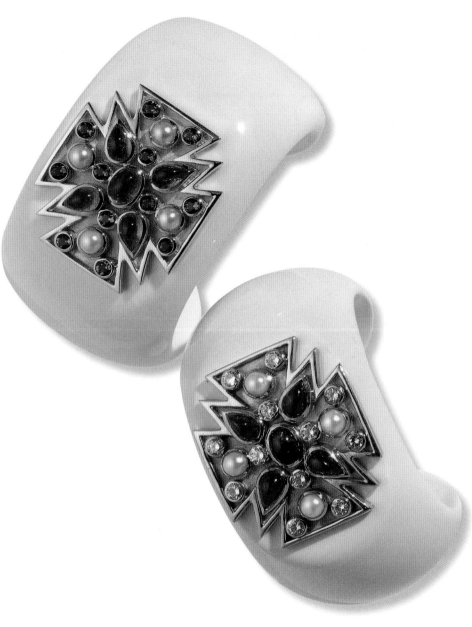

A cabochon ruby heart brooch by Verdura wrapped in a diamond ribbon.

fashion editor Diana Vreeland, introduced Verdura to Paul Flato, who hired him as a freelance designer. In 1939 Verdura opened his own upstairs boutique in New York with the financial backing of Vincent Astor and his good friend Cole Porter, who gave a funny little tribute to the designer in the 1941 song "Farming" from the show *Let's Face It:* "Liz Whitney has, on her bin of manure, a clip designed by the Duke of Verdura."

Blackamoors, tritons, gold rope, hearts, badges, and things with wings were the recurring motifs in the jewels Verdura designed that delighted his celebrity clientele. In 1941 silver-screen star Tyrone Power bought one of the designer's most romantic confections—a cabochon ruby heart brooch wrapped up in a gold ribbon. Leading man Gary Cooper chose a neo-Renaissance-style gold brooch for his wife in 1947 with a gold mermaid sitting on a rock splashed by sapphire waves. Betsey Cushing Whitney, wife of Jock Whitney, a Hollywood producer, fell in love with the little diamond-winged gold putti lounging on large turquoise cabochon brooches, festooned with diamond ribbons and pink topaz briolettes.

Both Millicent Rogers and the Duchess of Windsor had Verdura's signature shell brooches. The design consisted of real sea shells from the seashore—and the Museum of Natural History gift shop—studded with precious gems. When asked about the shells, Verdura confessed to *The New Yorker,* "What I get a kick out of is to buy a shell for five dollars, use half of it, and sell it for twenty-five hundred."

In 1972 Verdura sold his business to his partners and moved to London to follow the artistic pursuits of a gentleman. Painting had been a semiprofessional hobby for Verdura since the 1940s. He continued to paint his small landscapes and townscapes throughout his active retirement. Charming and amusing, the little works were exhibited and sold well. He also wrote a book about his childhood in Palermo called *The Happy Summer Days.* The year after it was published, Verdura passed away. Edward Landrigan bought the firm in 1984. The flair with which he has treated the Duke's jewelry and image has once again made Verdura a favorite of the fashion press and public.

ESTABLISHED: 1939
FOUNDER: Fulco di Verdura (1899–1978)
LOCATIONS: New York, Palm Beach

that made him a favorite in cafe society. When Elsa Maxwell compiled her list of twelve ideal dinner guests, she included Verdura along with Cole Porter, Maria Callas, Clare Boothe Luce, Somerset Maugham, and Noel Coward. The fact that Verdura was a titled Italian undoubtedly added to his social appeal.

Born a duke in Palermo in 1899, Verdura was a noble with little or no entitlement, according to the different versions of his life story. Verdura told *The New Yorker* in a 1941 interview that his father died in 1919 and left him a small inheritance that he spent "in riotous living" in Cannes, Venice, and Paris. He blew the last of his lira on a costume party at his family's villa before going to work. Verdura's obituary in *The London Times* gave another account. It said his father left him with a pile of debts when he died in 1926, forcing Verdura to go to work immediately. What the two stories do agree on is the fact that his first job was designing costume jewelry at Chanel, where he created a pair of Maltese cross cuffs that became a bestseller.

Verdura quit working at Chanel and moved to New York in 1934, where he did jewelry commissions for his friends, who were wealthy, witty, and well connected. One of them,

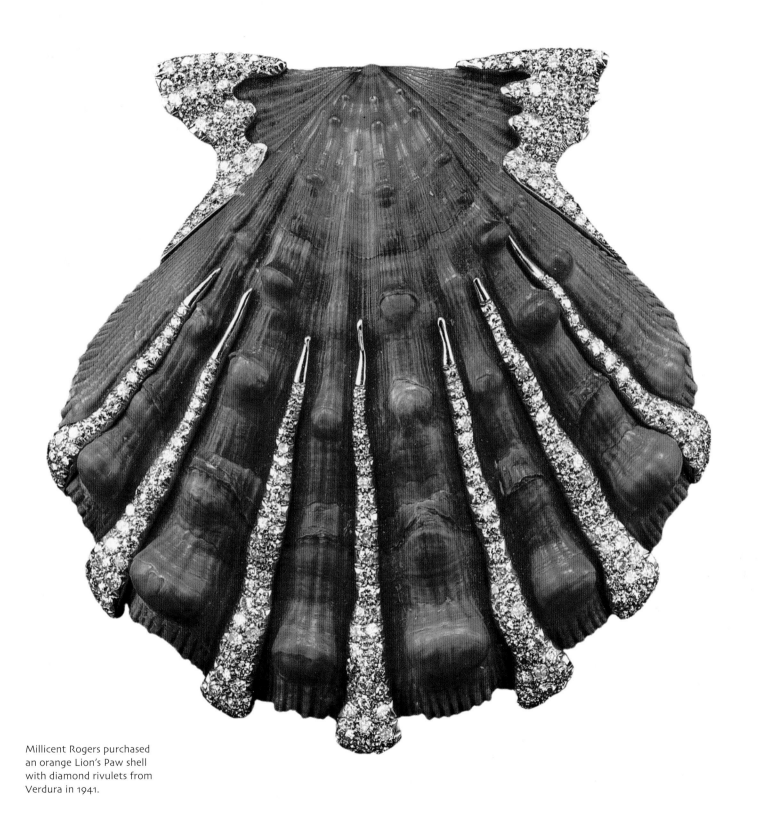

Millicent Rogers purchased
an orange Lion's Paw shell
with diamond rivulets from
Verdura in 1941.

SEAMAN SCHEPPS

Turbo shell earrings are without a doubt the design that made Seaman Schepps famous. They were a must-have for women with deep jewelry boxes like the Duchess of Windsor, Betsey Whitney, and Babe Paley since they debuted in the late 1930s. The twist to this success story is that Seaman Schepps did not create all of these ladies' turbo shell earrings: many of his contemporaries copied the design. The sheer number of imitators, beginning with Darde & Fils in the forties and on up to David Webb in the sixties, must have rankled Schepps, but he handled the situation breezily. Schepps liked to joke that the proliferation of turbo shell jewelry began when a quirky client brought one pair of beach shells to him and another pair to Verdura and asked both jewelers to "make her something." "Lo and behold," Schepps teased, "We both came up with the same design." (The design was actually created after a client brought Schepps a necklace of turbo shells from the Indian Ocean that she wanted made into earrings. The original pair had little cabochon turquoise and coral studding the shell that was mounted from north to south and wrapped in a gold wire.)

The turbo shell tale reveals a lot about Seaman Schepps's character. He had a fun-loving attitude about life that extended to his colleagues and his competitors. Schepps openly praised jewelers he admired such as Suzanne Belperron, Paul Flato, and Verdura. And he loved to joke about the ones who admired him. Schepps liked to tell a story about how David Webb used to linger outside his window when he was an up-and-coming jewelry designer looking for ideas. One day he stood there so long that Schepps went outside and said, "David, would you like a chair?"

Schepps began designing jewelry at forty-eight years old, after spending half a lifetime as a salesman, manager, and owner of jewelry stores in Los Angeles, San Francisco, and New York. His debut as a designer coincided with the 1929 stock market crash. The hard times encouraged his passion for mixing precious gems with materials of little value. He had been fascinated by the idea since a 1926 trip to Paris when he saw and fell in love with Suzanne Belperron's imaginative jewelry. Schepps's take on the concept, however, was very different than Belperron's refined designs. "He didn't mind mixing good stones with terrible stones, as long as it looked great," explained Patricia Vaill, Schepps's daughter, in a 1980s article for *Interview*.

Seaman Schepps made these turbo shell earrings accented with gold wire and emerald cabochons in 1949.

Jinx Falkenburg modeled her Seaman Schepps gold curb link choker with less-than-perfect cabochon sapphires, rubies, emeralds, and faceted amethysts and citrines on a 1948 cover of *Look*.

Schepps scavenged high and low for unusual things to add to his jewelry. In 1955 during a trip to Hong Kong, Schepps and his wife, Nell, abandoned the tour group they were with so he could prowl the Asian flea markets for coral, jade, and ivory statuettes—a few of these treasures became part of Schepps's Goddess of Heaven brooches. His collage type of work attracted women like Lauren Bacall, Joan Fontaine, Ann Sheridan, Gloria Vanderbilt, Blanche Knopf, and television and radio star Jinx Falkenburg, who wanted something spectacularly different.

Seaman Schepps retired in the late 1960s and turned the business over to his daughters, Patricia Vaill (1918–1992) and Virginia Jane. Patricia kept alive her father's aesthetic. "I used a lot of Daddy's ideas. But I would put my own little innovations into them. Then there are a few things that I have done that he had never thought of doing. But they are more or less a piece of his work. He is the only jeweler I copy," explained Vaill in *Interview*. The Schepps family sold the business to jewelers Anthony Hopenhajm and Jay Bauer in 1992. Hopenjam and Bauer make jewels from the firm's archive of twenty-two sketchbooks and thousands of renderings.

ESTABLISHED: Between 1904 and 1929 Schepps opened and closed three stores with various types of jewelry, one in Los Angeles, one in San Francisco, and one in New York. When he opened a New York boutique in 1934, the inventory changed to signature Schepps jewelry.
FOUNDER: Seaman Schepps (1881–1972)
LOCATION: New York

SCHLUMBERGER

Jean Schlumberger considered himself an anomaly in his field. Working in the late 1950s, he felt out of sync with other jewelers. "It's very complicated," he told Daniel Behrman, a reporter for *Réalités* in 1957, "I make jewels, but I hate modern jewelry—and I can't tell people I make antique jewels." Modern jewelry for Schlumberger meant matching suites of diamond and platinum jewelry set in abstract patterns. He described the look as "mainly a display of cash value."

Schlumberger's designs of sea creatures, fantasy flowers, and heraldic beasts, in contrast, were filled with colorful gems set in his signature goldwork with prickly frond details. Closer in spirit to representational Renaissance jewelry than anything in the modern mode, Schlumberger drew inspiration for his

A Goddess of Heaven brooch by Seaman Schepps features a carved aquamarine statuette standing on a large pink tourmaline rock. The ruby and diamond headpiece and bouquet of flowers come from antique jewels.

101

Jean Schlumberger in 1956.

The sapphire and diamond blossoms on the gold Morning Glory necklace by Schlumberger are wide open to the light.

jeweled flights of fancy from a library with illustrated volumes on lace, plants, flowers, and fish.

A self-taught designer, Schlumberger made a point of being honest with reporters, telling them upfront that he had no formal art training. "My mother had a saying, 'If you have something, it will come out some day,'" he said in a 1950s interview. "This may be true, but it would have been easier with art training." Born into a well-to-do French family of textile merchants, Schlumberger went through a series of design jobs before he landed in jewelry. He designed textiles in the United States, posters for a book publisher in France, and perfume packaging for the famous French couturier Lelong. When Lelong fired Schlumberger on the grounds that he did not show any potential, legend has it that the depressed designer headed to the flea market for solace and found one-hundred and twenty Dresden flowers made of china that he transformed into little brooches. The novelties caught the

attention of avant-garde couturier Elsa Schiaparelli who hired Schlumberger as a byline designer in 1938, giving his roller skate brooches, flying fish earrings, and other follies the credit line, "Schlumberger for Schiaparelli."

Schlumberger's service in the French Army and de Gaulle's Free French forces during World War II put his design career on hold. When peace was declared, he moved to New York and opened a precious jewelry firm in a townhouse at 21 East Sixty-third Street with a partner, Nicolas Bongard, the nephew of Jeanne Boivin, who had jewelry experience working for his aunt.

The art of Salvador Dalí and the surrealists influenced Schlumberger's early precious jewelry. His designs were as provocative, edgy, and haunting as jewelry can be. One strangely beautiful brooch made for Millicent Rogers in 1947 centers on a pink morganite stuck in a bed of thorns tied up with strips of fabric set with canary and white diamonds. A companion piece made for Rogers the same year was a similar thorn bush brooch with diamonds scattered in the branches and a light blue sapphire caught in the center.

After nine successful years with his own firm, Schlumberger became a byline designer at Tiffany & Co., where his designs subtly changed. He may have been influenced by the tailored Tiffany style, he may have mellowed with maturity, or simply shifted with the fashions. Whatever the case, Schlumberger's work became gentler and more feminine.

A dazzling piece of evening wear, the Morning Glory necklace of 1957 is a showpiece of Schlumberger's Tiffany style. It displays his artistic use of gems. A handful of sapphires highlighted with five irregular lines of diamonds make up each blossom and burst from the flamboyant gold vine mounting which is an integral part of the design. The vine's loops, twists, and turns put the large piece in motion. The overall effect, this wild growth of stems and blooms, is closer to something planned by Mother Nature than to the symmetry of most nature theme jewelry.

Among his daytime jewelry, Schlumberger's enamel bangles were the design of choice among the chic women of the early sixties. Bunny Mellon and Babe Paley purchased several, as did Jackie Kennedy, who wore hers so often the press dubbed the jewels, "Jackie Bangles." These everyday jewels had a not-so-everyday enamel technique called Paillonné. A complicated, labor-intensive process, executed by craftsmen in the Pyranees who had the specialized knowledge, Paillonné involved multiple firings of enamel on gold. This original use of

Jackie Kennedy in her signature accessories of the sixties: large sunglasses and an enamel bangle and earrings by Schlumberger.

Enamel bangles by Schlumberger are decorated with gold patterns. Some have gems as well.

Richard Burton with Elizabeth Taylor, who's wearing her Night of the Iguana brooch by Schlumberger, in front of their private jet in 1967.

Elizabeth Taylor's diamond, platinum, and gold Night of the Iguana brooch by Schlumberger has cabochon sapphire eyes and emerald lips.

an old enamel technique reflected Schlumberger's appreciation for jewelry history. In Diana Vreeland's 1976 book, *Jean Schlumberger: Bijoux*, she wrote about the bangles: "It was really Schlum who revived enamel, a 19th-century art we hadn't seen at all in the 20th century. His enamel is perfection. Clear, transparent sun yellows. Wonderful lacquer reds. Acid spring greens. The clear blue of the southern sky. He likes to stab enamel with nails of gold, as if to hold it from flying back to the world of nature from which he's taken its color. Like the direct eyes of a beast approaching you, the nails seem to say, 'The world is tough—and wonderful.'"

Schlumberger made thousands of drawings throughout his life and he received a lot of attention for his artistry. In the late fifties and early sixties, Schlumberger jewels inspired imaginative spreads in *Vogue* and *Harper's Bazaar*. In 1957 Schlumberger became the first jeweler to receive a Coty Award. In 1976, the French Government made him a Chevalier of the National Order of Merit. The treasure of designs Schlumberger left for Tiffany

when he passed away in 1987 has kept his legacy vibrantly alive. Pierce MacGuire, who took over the department in 1992, has delved deeply into the archives and produced magnificent designs that had never been manufactured before.

DATES: In 1940, Schlumberger established his firm in New York. He closed after one year to serve in the Free French Forces. In 1948 he reopened. He joined Tiffany in 1956.

FOUNDER: Jean Schlumberger (1907–1987)

BOOKS: Chantel Bizot, Evelyne Possémé, and Marie-Noël Gary. *The Jewels of Jean Schlumberger.* New York: Harry N. Abrams, Inc., 2001. Jean Schlumberger. *Bijoux,* preface by Diana Vreeland. Milan: Franco Maria Ricci, 1976; *Jean Schlumberger: Objets* preface by Jean d'Ormesson. Milan: Franco Maria Ricci, 1976.

EXHIBITION: 1995, Paris. *Un Diamond Dans La Ville*, Musée des Arts Décoratifs.

LOCATION: Schlumberger is sold at Tiffany & Co. stores.

DAVID WEBB

In the 1960s the fashion press was all ears when David Webb, a hot young designer, spoke his mind. He told columnist Ruth Preston: "What's wanted is the effect of tremendous glamour, not of tremendous value; a soft look rather than a stiff hardness of big stones just sitting around." Webb's own glamorous statement consisted of large animal bangle bracelets and brooches slathered in enamel and accented with precious gems. Zebras, horses, owls, frogs, and giraffes were just a few of the animals in Webb's kingdom. He said, "We've had the sweet things, the flowers and the little arrangements. It is time for boldness and simplicity. Animals are here to stay."

The animal jewels, an idea that came to Webb when he was sick in bed, won him a prestigious Coty award, coverage in *Vogue* and *Harper's Bazaar,* as well as a feature in the December 4, 1964 issue of *Life.* The success of the animals took Webb all the way to the White House. President John Kennedy and the First Lady Jackie Kennedy—who was a fan and client—commissioned him to design the Freedom Medal and to create objects with American gemstones for gifts of state. A stampede of high-profile animal lovers—including Diana Vreeland, the Duchess of Windsor, and Elizabeth Taylor—to Webb's boutique made him one of the biggest celebrity jewelers of the decade. "This stuff is not just ordinary diamonds-and-rubies junk," Taylor said of Webb's jewelry in a 1968 *Cosmopolitan* interview. " This is now—it's very chic."

David Webb's stellar success was in stark contrast to his humble beginnings. His first experience with metalwork was as a nine-year-old when he took a crafts course at a WPA school near his home in Asheville, North Carolina. He picked up the skills of goldsmithing and gemsetting from his father, grandfather, and uncle. At seventeen, Webb left home to apprentice in New York, often switching jobs to learn as much as he could about his craft from various workshops. After serving in the army during World War II, he started his own business in 1948 with Nina Silberstein creating jewelry in the prevailing Harry Winston and Van Cleef & Arpels modes.

Slowly he developed his own style that was a little younger and more fashion forward, a look that launched him in the movies. Webb's formal jewelry made Hollywood appearances on Doris Day in *Pillow Talk* (1959) and *Midnight Lace* (1960). Susan Hayward flaunted $1,150,000 worth of Webb jewelry in *Back Street* (1961), and within a week of the film's debut the entire collection sold out.

Richard Burton arrives at the Los Angles airport in 1967 with Elizabeth Taylor, who is wearing a brooch, ring, and animal bangle by David Webb.

Diana Vreeland's black and white enamel zebra bracelet by David Webb has diamond details and ruby eyes.

The Duchess of Windsor's green enamel, ruby, gold, and diamond frog bangle by David Webb was made in 1964.

A pavé-set diamond and gold turtle compact by David Webb has emerald eyes and a real tortoise's shell for a lid.

What put him on top was his artistic breakthrough with the animal jewels. This triumph was followed in 1970 by the success of his innovative crystal jewelry. For this line, Gloria Vanderbilt was his muse. Her long Art Deco crystal necklace from a Greenwich Village antique store inspired a discussion between jeweler and client at a Christmas party on the vulgarity of ostentatious jewelry and the beauty of low-key luxury design. The next day, on a flight to Australia, Webb began designing a crystal collection. About twenty hours later, upon arrival in Sydney, he had twelve drawings ready for his workshop.

Webb's inspiration for his crystal pieces came from his mental library of images built up over the years spent at the Metropolitan Museum of Art. Byzantine art influenced the design of his carved crystal and gold cross. Art Deco jewelry gave Webb the blueprint for a bombé-shaped cocktail ring in carved crystal. Fashion journalist Marian Christy reported on the crystal collection in April, 1970, "The new jewelry, set in gold or platinum and studded with tiny diamonds is the perfect answer of what to wear with sportive clothes. Besides, it doesn't scream the fact that the wearer has unlimited means. Crystal looks like glass."

David Webb died of cancer in 1975 at fifty years old. The Silberstein family has continued the firm. Prolific in his output of jewelry designs, Webb left a wealth of material for the Silbersteins to produce.

ESTABLISHED: 1946
FOUNDER: David Webb (1925–1975)
LOCATION: New York
MOVIE CREDITS: *Pillow Talk* (1959), *Midnight Lace* (1960), and *Back Street* (1961)

A few diamonds sparkle among the faceted pieces of rock crystal in a long gold necklace designed by David Webb in the 1970s.

THE MINIMALISTS

When women were stepping into professional positions en masse during the seventies and early eighties, they not only had to learn how to make it in a man's world, but how to dress in it, too. For women in creative fields—editors, art directors, and TV producers—the dress code was suits with clean, lean lines. When it came to jewelry this stylish crowd chose minimal metal looks by Elsa Peretti and Robert Lee Morris that were sleek accents on modern monochromatic clothes.

The exceptional way in which Elsa Peretti and Robert Lee Morris jewelry coordinated with clothes led both to long-term associations with top New York fashion designers who created pieces with the working woman in mind. Peretti collaborated with Halston and Giorgio di Sant'Angelo in the 1970s, and Morris did accessories for Donna Karan during the 1980s. In the 1990s, when fashion minimalism swung around again, the new and old collections of Peretti and Morris experienced a huge resurgence in popularity and became award-winning styles. Robert Lee Morris won the prestigious CFDA Accessory Designer of the Year award in 1994 for his body of work. Two years later Elsa Peretti received the same award for designs she had created over twenty years before. A new generation had discovered these masters of minimalist jewelry and found them totally cool.

ELSA PERETTI

"I design for the working girl," explained Elsa Peretti in a 1974 interview with *People* magazine shortly after her launch party at Tiffany that attracted over two thousand fans. "What I want is not to become a status symbol but to give beauty at a price." Her collection brought down significantly the high price of jewelry at Tiffany with pieces for as little as $33. The smallest version of her diamond necklace called "Diamonds by the Yard" cost $89 in 1974. Peretti's jewelry put Tiffany in touch with what

was happening on the street. The economic crunch was part of it. The other part was the increasingly casual fashions. The line she made with the working girl in mind was also a big hit with the elite Ultrasuaves, a nickname for trendsetting women, like actress Liza Minnelli, art collector Ethel Scull, and *Vogue* editor-in-chief Grace Mirabella, who wore Halston Ultrasuede.

How an Italian designer changed America's most celebrated jewelry store overnight is a story with twists and turns. The daughter of Maria Luigia and Ferdinando Peretti, founder of the API oil company, Elsa Peretti was born in 1940 in Florence and brought up in an atmosphere of privilege. At twenty-one, she left home to teach languages and skiing at her old Swiss boarding school. Next she got an interior design degree in Rome and worked for an architect in Milan. In 1966, Peretti relocated to Barcelona where she became a model and, as she puts it, "began to create the basis for a different approach to life." Two years later she moved to New York City. "I arrived in New York. There was a garbage strike and I thought I was in hell," remembers Peretti. "Then I met Giorgio di Sant'Angelo." A top Italian fashion designer working in New York, di Sant'Angelo and Peretti became fast friends and she

Liza Minnelli wearing two Bone cuffs by Elsa Peretti in the 1970s.

The Open Heart, Flask, Tear Drop, and Bean pendants and two Bone cuffs show off Elsa Peretti's spare sculptural style.

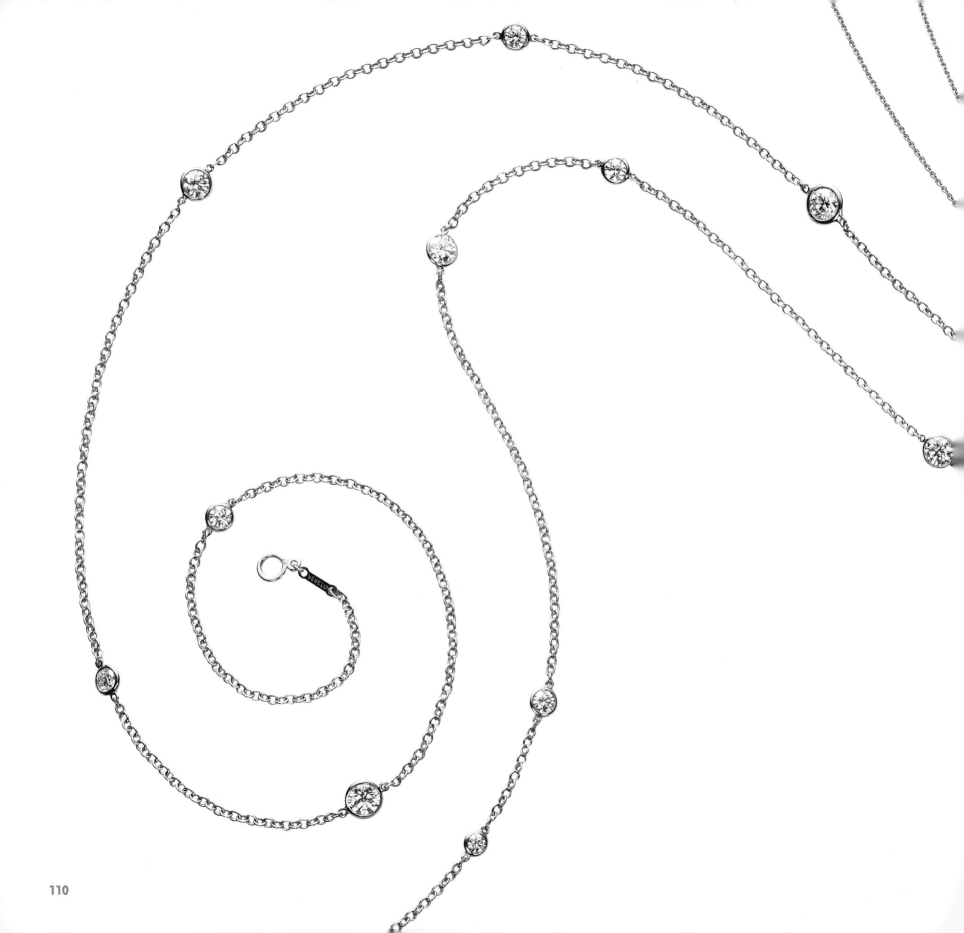

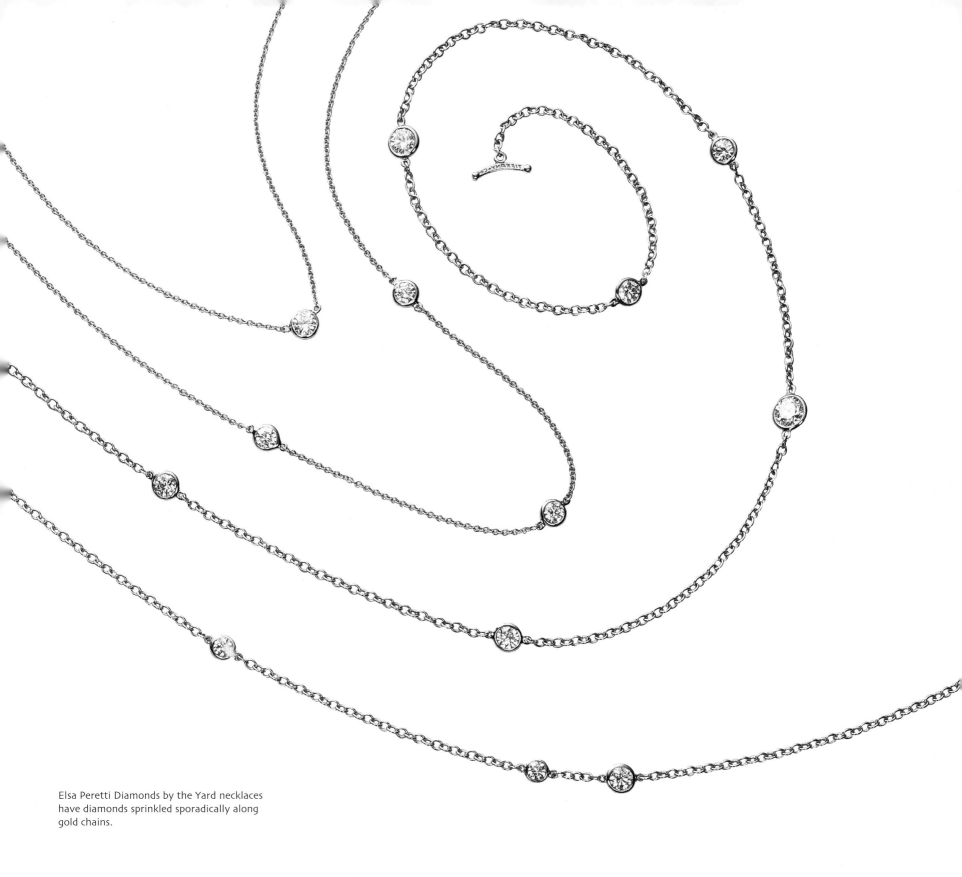

Elsa Peretti Diamonds by the Yard necklaces have diamonds sprinkled sporadically along gold chains.

A 1970s fashion photograph of models in Halston clothes. Elsa Peretti (second from left) wears a snake belt she designed.

Silver jewelry with shapely curves like the ones on Peretti's Bottle have defined a major portion of her work at Tiffany. Her signature triumpherate of pendants, the Bean, the Open Heart, and the Teardrop, are all characterized by delicately voluptuous contours. The Bone Cuff, another Peretti perennial, has a modulated incline that glides over the wrist bone. Perretti's slightly sinister Scorpion necklace and Snake collection are built up of smooth articulated shells and scales so cleverly executed that the designs look abstract at first glance.

Peretti says the ideas for her jewelry just come to her. "It's part of being a designer," she explains. "You think about your time and life and other people, and then you make jewelry that is easy for them to wear." Peretti sketches designs, then works closely with her craftsman on the bench, adjusting things and perfecting details as the manufacturing goes along and the jewel evolves. For a couple of collections the designer has worked with jewelry historians and master craftsmen for insight into old techniques such as lacquer, mesh, and basket weaving to apply to her designs.

Compared to her disco days in New York in the seventies, Elsa Peretti has a much quieter life, working and living mainly in Spain, in the small Catalan village of Sant Martí Vell. Her jewelry, however, still shines in the limelight. Hollywood actresses Gwyneth Paltrow, Jodie Foster, and Jennifer Aniston have replaced the Ultrasuaves as the high-profile women who wear her designs. And the number of working girls that adore her jewelry has never diminished. For over a quarter of a century at Tiffany, Peretti has remained remarkably focused and the jewelry that seemed to some like a trendy fashion statement in the beginning has magnificently withstood the test of time.

found herself at the very center of the happening fashion scene. Working as a model, she became a favorite of photographer Helmut Newton and a muse and close friend of Halston. All the while, Peretti was still searching for a way to express her own creativity. When she discovered what she wanted to do, she told di Sant'Angelo, "It's going to be jewelry." Though the decision seemed somewhat spontaneous, her first jewels—an organic bottle pendant and heart-shaped belt—were an instant success when di Sant'Angelo and Halston both showed them on their runways. "A lot of people liked the bottle," says Peretti, "and I continued to model to pay for the production."

In 1972 Peretti's collection was picked up by Bloomingdale's. The department store organized Cul de Sac, a special boutique to showcase Peretti's work and that of other up-and-coming young designers, including David Yurman and M+J Savitt. Two years later Peretti made the move to Tiffany. "It all happened when George O'Brian, the art director at Tiffany, spoke to [fashion editor] Carrie Donovan, who spoke to Halston, who spoke to me, and set up the meeting," says Peretti. She showed the Tiffany executives her Bottle pendant and then immediately signed a contract to work for the jeweler.

DESIGNER: Elsa Peretti (born 1940)
BOOK: Peretti, Elsa and Florencio Palencia, *Fifteen of my Fifty with Tiffany*, Spain, 1990.
EXHIBITIONS: 1990, New York. *Elsa Peretti: Fifteen of My Fifty with Tiffany*, Fashion Institute of Technology, April 24–May 10, 1990.
LOCATIONS: Elsa Peretti jewelry is sold at Tiffany & Co. stores.

Elsa Peretti works on jewelry at a butcher block table in her New York City apartment in 1974 wearing Diamonds by the Yard with a blouse and black leather apron made for her by Halston.

A sensuously sculpted scorpion necklace by Elsa Peretti.

ROBERT LEE MORRIS

When Robert Lee Morris opened Artwear in 1977, the store instantly became a part of the happening New York City scene. His jewelry and the work of like-minded designers, Ted Muehling, Patricia Von Musulin, and Cara Croninger, was shown on sexy plaster casts of male and female torsos described by the *New York Times* as "startling." The *Saturday Night Fever* soundtrack was pumped through the stereo system onto the sidewalk to lure customers into the party atmosphere. "The energy of the jewelry matched the energy of the clubs," remembers Morris.

Artwear originally opened on the Upper East Side, but despite extensive attention from the press and steady sales to luminaries like Gianni Agnelli, who bought golden masks and long, golden finger talons to wear at Studio 54, Morris could not keep up with the exorbitant rent for his Madison Avenue store. "After six months I got out of my lease and moved to Soho." The new location put Artwear at the heart of the avant-garde art world. "From the moment we opened our doors, there were huge crowds," Morris explains. "We were the hottest store in New York for over a decade."

The concept of Artwear, an enterprise of creative people, was a natural evolution from Morris's hippie past. After graduating from Beloit College in Wisconsin in 1969, he formed a craft commune, Big Ted's Farm, with some college friends. "Everyone on the farm made something different— pottery, sweaters, macramé," says Morris. "I decided to make jewelry. I got a book called *How to Make Jewelry* by Thomas Gentile, which was easy to follow with lots of pictures. I said to myself, I need a hammer and some wire, and I built a workshop in the tool shed. I would listen to Led Zeppelin's first album and work until two or three o'clock in the morning in total ecstasy."

After a fire burned the farm down, Morris sold his jewelry at craft fairs and at a little store he opened in Vermont. The designer stepped into a much larger arena in 1971 when Joan Sonnabend bought his pieces for her Sculpture to Wear boutique in New York City's Plaza Hotel, which featured jewelry by Pablo Picasso, Louise Nevelson, and Man Ray. Unfortunately, Sculpture to Wear closed shortly after Morris relocated to New York City. In search of a retail outlet, he took a selection of his jewelry, which was neither precious nor costume but an artistic fashion statement, to several possible places. Art dealer Leo Castelli asked, "What am I going to do with it?" Buyers at

the department store Bergdorf Goodman could not figure out where to place it on the sales floor. The gap in the marketplace for artistic accessories of this kind, and the plight of other adventurous jewelers, inspired Morris to establish Artwear.

Two years after the store opened, Morris's reputation as a creator of outlandish, often hard-to-wear jewelry, was transformed and he became the fashion world's darling who did accessories that were right on target every season. His experience with fashion designers began when Geoffrey Beene asked him to accessorize his runway show in 1979. Over the next five years Morris collaborated with Calvin Klein, Kansai Yamamoto, Anne Klein's designer Louis Dell'Olio, and Karl Lagerfeld. In 1985 he started working with Donna Karan, and his position in the fashion world was secured.

The impact of Donna Karan's new body-conscious clothing, lit up by Morris's jewelry, was felt at her first show. Silver and gold vermeil bead necklaces, Maasai-style collars, organically-shaped big round earrings, and mega cuffs went perfectly with Karan's wide shoulders, elongated torso, and cinched-waist ensembles made out of wool jersey in a black palette. The first collection Morris did with Karan was honored by the fashion industry with a CFDA for accessories. Morris then received his second CFDA in 1994. At the ceremony, parts of which were aired on CNN, the designer electrified the audience with his acceptance speech when he proclaimed, "Fashion without jewelry is like sex without orgasm!"

Robert Lee Morris sits in front of torsos displaying his jewelry at Artwear in 1984.

Silver jewelry by Robert Lee Morris.

Donna Karen accessorized her
1985 debut collection with silver
jewelry by Robert Lee Morris.

Robert Lee Morris's links to the fashion world influenced the way he designed. He produced lines of jewelry on a seasonal schedule, quickly changing his metals, colors, and proportions with the trends. Jewelry from antiquity, especially Celtic, ethnic styles, the female form, and organic shapes are the threads that unify all his work. "My forms are soft and they have undulations to them," says Morris. "My jewelry is just a little rounder or thicker than normal. It has extra voluptuousness to it."

The designer reached a turning point in 1995, the year "Metalmania: A 25-Year Retrospective Exhibition of the Work and Career of Robert Lee Morris" at the Museum at the Fashion Institute of Technology. "It was like a punctuation point in my career," says Morris. "It made me realize I wanted to do something different." Three years later he formed a partnership with M. Fabrikant & Sons, a large gem supplier and manufacturer, which made it possible for Morris to begin designing with precious materials.

The minutiae of nature, things usually overlooked, sent Morris to the drawing board for his fine jewelry line. His view of the great outdoors was closer to the ecological movement, with its concerns about preservation, than to the traditional perspective of nature in jewelry, which depicted flowers and bugs in a straightforward way. A section of a spider web inspired Morris to create a reversible bib of platinum threads and large platinum dewdrops with diamond centers on one side and pearl centers on the other. Pebbles from a riverbed prompted him to make thick round gold pendants, rings, and earrings with gentle depressions where he placed a pearl.

Morris balances his past and present to forge ahead for the future. The vintage designs he still produces—oversize collars, bangles, hoops, and big rings—are almost perpetually hot with the fashion flock and celebrities like Lauryn Hill and Janet Jackson, who are looking for a bold gold or silver look. As for the precious part of the designer's work, Morris's fresh approach has generated a wave of enthusiasm and he has been honored with many awards by the fine jewelry industry.

ESTABLISHED: 1970
FOUNDER: Robert Lee Morris (born 1947)
EXHIBITION: 1995, New York. *Metalmania: A 25-Year Retrospective Exhibition of the Work and Career of Robert Lee Morris*. The Museum at the Fashion Institute of Technology.
LOCATIONS: Artwear (1977–1993), the Robert Lee Morris Gallery (established in 1983), both in New York. Morris's jewelry is also available at department stores.

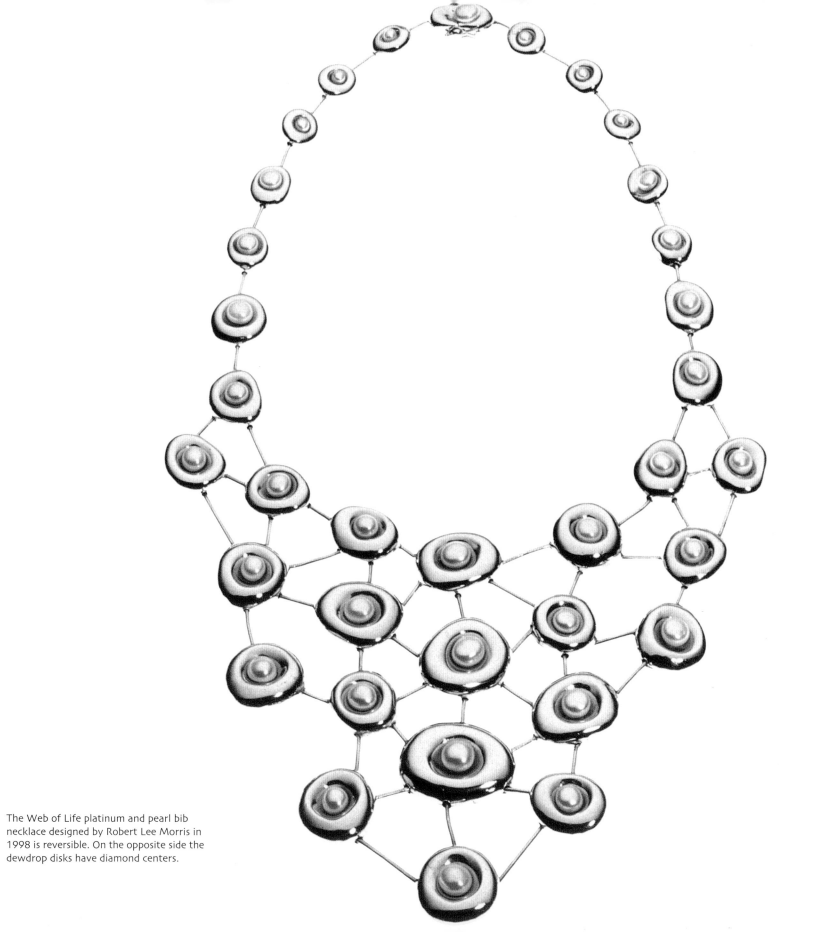

The Web of Life platinum and pearl bib
necklace designed by Robert Lee Morris in
1998 is reversible. On the opposite side the
dewdrop disks have diamond centers.

SIGNATURE STYLISTS

During the long run of the bull market in the 1980s, the appetite for designer goods was at an all-time high. The most desirable items were ones that broadcast the maker's name. A woman who shopped at Chanel left no doubt as to where she was buying her wardrobe. The firm's designer, Karl Lagerfeld, took logo mania to an extreme by putting the Chanel interlocked "C" logo all over everything from buttons to sunglasses to sneakers.

In this flashy fashion era jewelers made their work stand out by creating bold designs, unique motifs, and special finishes that were the equivalent of a logo. Some of the most recognizable designs came from Paloma Picasso, David Yurman, and Barry Kieselstein-Cord. These jewelers created distinctive looks and turned their names and jewels into status symbols with modern business savvy. They built empires on strategies planned to satisfy the feeding frenzy for brand names. Advertising and courting editors assured coverage in magazines. Kieselstein-Cord and Yurman sold their lines at luxury department stores, establishing their jewels as part of the one-stop shopping experience.

The strong images built by all three designers inspired them to do accessories beyond jewelry, like belts, handbags with fancy hardware, and watches. These ventures provided the faithful with fresh choices and furthered the worldwide recognition of the designers' signature styles. Savvy in business as well as design, Picasso, Yurman, and Kieselstein-Cord went after imitators who knocked off their popular and usually patented accessories with a vengeance. Legal action protected the original designs from a sea of look-alikes and stopped the predatory competition from taking a bite out of profits. By the time the economy and fashion changed in the early 1990s, signature looks from the three designers had entered the catalogue of twentieth-century jewelry hits.

PALOMA PICASSO

When Paloma Picasso debuted her first collection for Tiffany in 1980, *Vogue* said, "It redefined 'real' jewelry in a modern sense." At a time when "real" jewelry was expected to have diamonds, Picasso designed with semiprecious stones. The sophisticated way she handled the gems gave them cache. "She would take a citrine and make it look as important as a canary diamond," says legendary *Vogue* accessories editor Candy Pratts Price.

What the press saw as a bold move away from diamond jewelry was intuitive for Picasso. "I like big stones," she explains. "And with semiprecious stones you can work in really large sizes." A few of the heavier carat weights that have appeared in Picasso jewelry were a 52.62-carat kunzite and a 284-carat peridot. The wide range of colors available in semiprecious stones was just as important to Picasso as size. She says, "I guess that comes from being the child of two painters."

The youngest daughter of Pablo Picasso and Françoise Gilot, Paloma Picasso remembers thinking about aesthetics as early as age twelve, and jewelry was very much a part of her musings. "When I was young, I would often ask my mother if I could review her jewelry with her," says Picasso. She got her first professional experience in jewelry in 1968, designing costume pieces for a Paris theater production. Then she did a collection of costume jewelry for Yves Saint-Laurent. Picasso mastered the fundamentals of precious jewelry by taking courses at a Paris jewelry school. After that she did special commissions

"Paloma designed these especially for me."

A 1995 *New Yorker* cartoon.

Picasso's gestural style shines
through her signature designs:
a Scribble brooch; an X pendant;
a Love and Kisses brooch;
and a Loving Hearts ring.

for friends and a few pieces for the Greek jeweler Zolotas. By the tail end of the seventies Picasso was a well-respected figure in the French fashion world with talent and an eye for talent. Manolo Blahnik, the shoe designer, credits her with opening up his career when she introduced him to *Vogue* fashion editor Diana Vreeland. Her own career leapt to an international level when Tiffany design director John Loring asked her to join the firm in 1980. Loring says he chose Picasso because he felt "her love of ample scale and strong color would be a perfect vehicle to perpetuate Tiffany's traditional supremacy in semiprecious stones."

If Charles Lewis Tiffany, Louis Comfort Tiffany, and gemologist George Kunz, the men who established the firm's reputation for fine work with semiprecious stones in the early years of the twentieth century, could see Picasso's semiprecious jewelry, they would be delighted that a rock hound was firmly in place at Tiffany again. But they would not recognize Picasso's style, since it did not derive from historical sources. A bolt of lightning and a thunderstorm inspired Picasso to place a 408.63-carat moonstone, the color of an overcast storm sky, on a cutting edge-diamond and gold bracelet with a dramatic zigzag pattern. For a thoroughly modern statement jewel from 1986, Picasso wrapped a 396.30-carat kunzite in billowing diamond ribbons, which curled around a necklace of misshapen South Sea baroque pearls.

Big bold jewels with semiprecious stones were almost all Picasso did during her first few years at Tiffany. They established a strong image for the designer, but her signature style was not complete until around 1983 when she introduced the flip side to her luxury look. "I realized I should be doing something that was easier to manufacture, more accessible in price," says Picasso. The pieces she came up with were little personal expressions in silver and gold that became huge successes. Her Scribble brooch was inspired by the graffiti that was on the streets and subways in New York City during the eighties and a controversial part of the art world. "At the time everybody was talking against graffiti," says Picasso. "I thought, let's give a good name to graffiti." Her gestural X's—transformed into earrings, brooches, necklaces, and rings—came from the symbol for a kiss that she discovered as a teenager in England on her friends' love letters. "I'd never seen this, of course, and it stayed with me. I loved it," remembers Picasso.

During the high-rolling eighties, Picasso modeled her jewelry in Tiffany advertisements. Her strong look, bold

Paloma Picasso accessorizes a white suit with a large bead necklace.

jewelry, sharp clothes, and the deep red lipstick she called Mon Rouge, which she packaged and sold, made her a style icon and the subject of countless fashion magazine articles. This barrage of personal publicity combined with the popularity of her jewelry established the designer as an individual talent independent of her famous father. Her gemmy jewels and signature designs, symbols of art and love, are recognized as Paloma Picasso the world over.

DESIGNER: Paloma Picasso (born 1949)
ESTABLISHED: Picasso started designing jewelry exclusively for Tiffany in 1980.
FILM: *Black Widow* (1986)
LOCATIONS: Paloma Picasso jewelry is sold at Tiffany & Co. stores.

A baroque South Sea
pearl necklace designed
by Paloma Picasso
in 1986 suspends a
supersize 396.30-carat
kunzite wrapped in
diamond, platinum,
and gold ribbons.

(From left to right) Pierre Bergé, Lulu Klossowski, Yves Saint Laurent, Picasso, and Thadee Klossowski party together in 1981.

A gold ring with a large cabochon gem by Paloma Picasso.

An X choker by Paloma Picasso features green and pink tourmalines, aquamarine, amethysts, and citrines.

DAVID YURMAN

In 1981, after years of making figurative jewelry, David Yurman began experimenting with wire. "I was thinking, what can I do that is really simple using material just for material," explained Yurman. In 1982 he twisted fifty-two feet of gold strands into soft helix-shaped bracelets. "The design comes out of the history of art," says Yurman. "I was looking at ancient Egyptian jewelry." He made the age-old form modern by creating fashionable proportions and adding caps of semiprecious stones. When Yurman finished his first cable bracelets, he looked at them and said, "You have done it." The cable became Yurman's signature and over the years it has taken him from being a designer to a megabrand name.

The sculptural quality and the patinas of Yurman's cable are features that can be traced back to his artistic beginnings. When Yurman was a teenager in the early sixties, he apprenticed under several sculptors, including the Cubist Jacques Lipchitz. By age twenty he had a one-man show at a gallery in Great Neck, Long Island, and he continued to study sculpture at the Art Students League and the School of Visual Arts in New York.

Around 1969 Yurman met his soul mate and future wife, Sybil, who was an integral part of the shift in his career from sculpture to jewelry. It all began with a little bronze angel belt buckle he made for Sybil, who wore it to the Form Gallery in New York. "When the owner asked if it was for sale, David said no," remembers Sybil. "And I said yes." Yurman's first few pieces for the gallery quickly sold, and the couple took out a $500 loan from the Jewish Free Loan Society in order to create six molds for more belt buckles. Then they exhibited the collection on the craft fair circuit. "We cut logs and made giant easels to hang the belts on," recalls Yurman. "It was one of our early sales techniques that really worked."

Soon after, the couple expanded into jewelry. David handled the metalwork in bronze, silver, and gold. He welded the pieces, did the molds, and cast them. Sybil, who had studied painting, was responsible for creating the color schemes with beads. For one jewel she combined turquoise, chalcedony, and yellow pearls. After seven years of exhibiting at craft shows and galleries, the Yurmans moved on to fine-jewelry trade shows like the Retail Jewelers of America. "Even though we were crafting, we didn't fit into the craft world and it was time for a broader audience," said Yurman. Soon Yurman's jewelry began to take over a sizable amount of floor space in

Cubist sculptor Jacques Lipchitz with his young apprentice David Yurman in his studio in the early 1960s.

Neiman-Marcus, Bloomingdale's, and Saks Fifth Avenue. The jewelry that maintained his real estate in high end department stores was almost completely cable.

"The cable had the ability to build on itself," says Yurman. "It is a palette with endless possibilities." Over the years, he has changed the metals and gems, using precious and semi-precious stones, silver, and gold. He has also changed the amount of cable in his necklaces, bracelets, earrings, and rings, contrasting the twisted surface with a shiny smooth surface. "We modified our quintessential bracelet, model number 4157, like nine times," says Yurman. The variations were done in response to consumer demands. "We stay with our customer and watch what they are doing and wearing," he explains. "Sybil and I travel to Paris, Milan, and Sienna to look at what people are wearing. Then you squint your eyes and see almost what people aren't wearing and you see the colors you need in your next collection. It is reinvention through color and shape. And this is why I think we are successful, because the colors and the classic shaping of the jewelry are related to real moments."

After twenty years of making jewelry, the Yurmans find lots of different ways to keep their business fresh and lively. 1999 was a banner year with a series of successes. David and Sybil, who is president of the firm, opened their first boutique on Madison Avenue in New York City.

On the product front, Yurman extended his collections by launching a luxury watch line called the Thoroughbred for men and women. He and Sybil worked on the design and its twenty variations in enamel, silver, diamonds, and, of course, cable for over two years before it was introduced at the Basel Fair. A high point of the year was the return of the sculpted angel, the motif that jumpstarted the business, in the form of a pin Yurman made to help raise money and heighten awareness for Lou Gehrig's disease. Commenting on his charitable work, Yurman said in an interview with the *Boston Herald*, "I have enough money and enough fame, and I can only eat three meals a day. It's good to get outside, and do something that's not business as usual."

ESTABLISHED: 1971

FOUNDERS:: David and Sibyl Yurman

LOCATIONS: There is one David Yurman store in New York City. Yurman's jewelry is available at department stores and jewelry boutiques around the world.

Gem-accented Cable bracelets by David Yurman.

BARRY KIESELSTEIN-CORD

There is no simple way to describe Barry Kieselstein-Cord. He is internationally famous for his sculptural matte gold jewelry, but that's far from the whole of his reputation. He is just as well known for dramatic buckles and purses with whimsical hardware. The Metropolitan Museum of Art, the Louvre, and the Museum of Fine Arts, Houston all have Kieselstein-Cord belts and handbags in their collections. The designer is also an accomplished photographer. He shoots the ad campaigns for his company. He does exhibition-quality black-and-white photographs of landscapes, architectural details, and vintage cars in a style of a time gone by. When Kieselstein-Cord tries to describe himself, he says, "I am an artist who happens to own a luxury company." Later, in the same conversation he rephrases his description, "I have always felt I was a business person first, then an artist."

This tangle of terms is central to the story of Kieselstein-Cord. From the beginning, he has been super active in both the right and left side of the brain activities. When Kieselstein-Cord was studying at Parsons School of Design in New York City during the sixties, he channeled his creativity into commercial art, because, he says, "I didn't want to starve." Advertising absorbed his talents for seven years, until the field lost its appeal. "I got tired of selling panty hose and cigarettes and stuff I didn't believe in totally," explains Kieselstein-Cord. He quit the ad world, traveled all over England, Italy, and France, and set up an import-export business of small pieces he found in the flea markets abroad. During that time Kieselstein-Cord took a jewelry course for a few weeks with a girlfriend. "The school said I didn't have any talent in design," he remembers. "But a friend of mine, Michael Braun, [a set designer] said it was what I should be doing."

Encouraged by Braun's advice, Kieselstein-Cord began making sculptural butterfly- and horseshoe-shaped silver jewelry in 1972. The designs whipped up a small storm of enthusiasm. Georg Jensen, the boutique that had been the cradle for avant-garde silver jewelry designers since the early part of the century, showcased the collection. Then the specialty store Henri Bendel picked up the line. By 1977 Kieselstein-Cord was one of the hottest young jewelers in New York, part of a select group that sizzled in a *Newsweek* cover story "Jewelry's New Dazzle." In the feature the designer hinted where his muse would be taking him: "Jewelry has returned to being an art form."

Barry Kieselstein-Cord at Crocodile Hall, his 1920s mansion in New York City that serves as his office, showroom, and home.

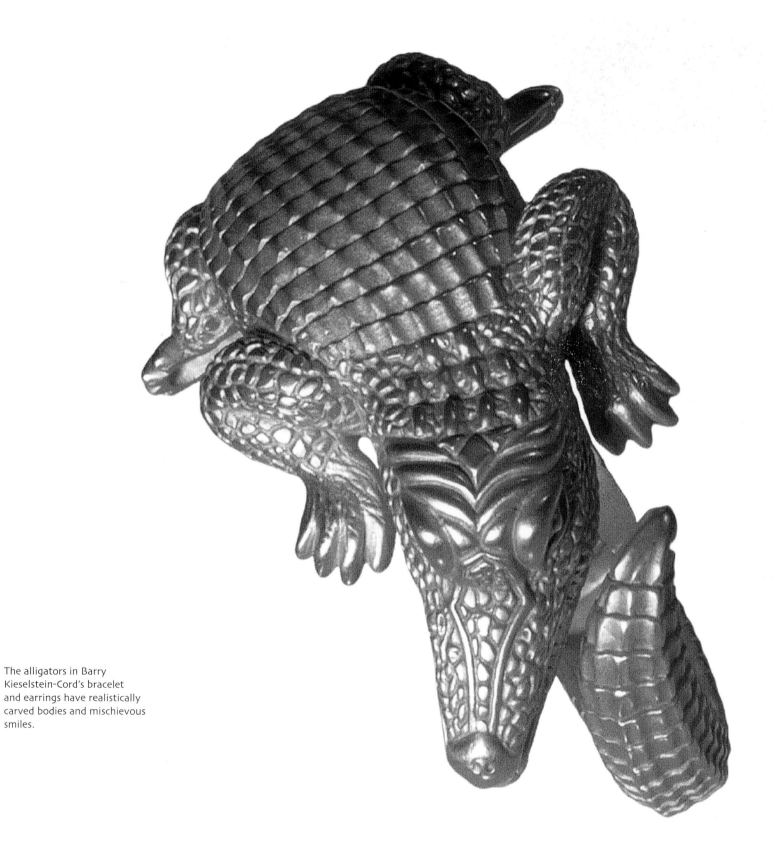

The alligators in Barry
Kieselstein-Cord's bracelet
and earrings have realistically
carved bodies and mischievous
smiles.

Sharon Stone wore
Kieselstein-Cord jewelry in
Basic Instinct (1992).

Kieselstein-Cord's love of antiques and art history inspired his work from the beginning. For the Pompeii collection, introduced in 1976, the designer looked at the luxury wares of the grand Roman city. "The richness of the culture stimulated me to create my fantasy of that period," he explains. "The pieces are in geometric shapes but with slight variations—it's as though the sands of time have worn down the pieces to create round corners."

The designer devised a special finish for the Pompeii collection that involved twenty-two steps and resulted in matte gold that was unlike anything else on the market at the time. For several years the matte gold jewelry sales were slow, but Kieselstein-Cord stuck with the style. He felt the patina gave his jewelry the feel of being old, used, and loved. When he moved his line from the New York City specialty store Henri Bendel to its neighbor, the upscale department store Bergdorf Goodman around 1981, the look finally took off.

In 1984 Kieselstein-Cord launched an intaglio collection, inspired by a family heirloom, a Roman intaglio ring that he wears practically every day. "The intaglio has a direct reference to gentry and a significant meaning," says Kieselstein-Cord. "They were used as seals for identification throughout the ancient world. Great artistry was devoted to these tiny delicate works of art." To recreate the look, Kieselstein-Cord had intaglios from original designs hand carved in rubies, sapphires, carnelians, tourmalines, and rhodolites by European craftsmen who knew the old procedures. The mountings for the engraved gems were unique designs, rearrangements of the elements of ancient architecture. Bracelets and rings were shaped like fluted columns with scrolled Ionic capitals.

Of all Kieselstein-Cord's signature jewels, the alligator bracelet has become the designer's icon. The creature is to Kieselstein-Cord what the panther is to Cartier, an unofficial mascot of the firm. Introduced in 1988, the inspiration for the carved gold gator that wraps around the wrist comes from one of Kieselstein-Cord's unusual childhood pets. "I had an alligator when I was a boy in Florida, which I kept in an ornamental pond," remembers Kieselstein-Cord. "For me, the alligator is a symbol of strength and cunning, and it's also a water symbol."

Kieselstein-Cord won the Coty American Fashion Critics Award two times, in 1979 and 1984, and the CFDA in 1981, but he does not consider himself part of the fashion milieu. He keeps every one of his collections in production and adds new ones as the spirit moves him. "I don't create for any specific time," says Kieselstein-Cord. "Many of my designs take up to four years to come to fruition so they are not typical of the moment." Nevertheless, his unmistakable look has attracted a very fashionable audience. Sharon Stone, Cher, Elizabeth Taylor, and Janet Jackson are just a few of his celebrity clients. Socialite Blaine Trump has worn her Kieselstein-Cord tourmaline and diamond pendant suspended from a multistrand pearl necklace at gala occasions for years. On top of doing the designing, Kieselstein-Cord runs his international company himself from his headquarters, Crocodile Hall, a 1920s mansion in New York City which is his home, showroom, and studio.

ESTABLISHED: 1972
FOUNDER: Barry Kieselstein-Cord
FILMS: *Basic Instinct* (1993), *Delores Claiborne* (1995)
LOCATIONS: Aspen, Palm Beach, Berlin, Zurich, and Dusselfdorf. The jewelry is also available at Bergdorf Goodman in New York and Neiman Marcus stores throughout the United States.

Blaine Trump wearing her Kieselstein-Cord necklace with a white dress.

Rings and bracelet from Kieselstein-Cord's Intaglio collection.

THE PRINCE OF PAVÉ

In the 1980s Joel Rosenthal, who signs his jewelry JAR, created a new style based on elements from the past. One-hundred-year-old gem cuts, nineteenth-century oxidized silver settings, unusual semiprecious stones that were popular with turn-of-the-century rock hounds, and the butterfly brooch, an Edwardian favorite, were all part of the JAR repertoire. These elements caused some people to label the jeweler a revivalist, but he was not. Rosenthal used the old materials in new ways. He masterfully mixed them up to create artistic effects in a signature pavé setting.

Rosenthal's pavé has created enthusiasm among jewelers in much the same way as René Lalique ignited the Art Nouveau designers. A handful of Rosenthal's contemporaries have worked out their own look around the elements the designer introduced. "I have been inspired by the new medium and vocabulary that JAR has brought to jewelry design," says Taffin designer James de Givenchy, who distinguishes his work from the master by making exuberant designs with platinum as opposed to silver. Others have perpetuated the JAR genre by superficially imitating the style.

The pavé movement has occurred although Rosenthal has done little to publicize his work. He does not loan jewelry to celebrities for red-carpet occasions or to magazines for fashion spreads. The designer prefers to artistically orchestrate how his jewelry is presented to the public. On his tenth anniversary in 1987, for example, he put together a one-night, by-invitation-only exhibition at the National Academy of Design in New York City. Because he believes his work says everything, Rosenthal rarely gives interviews. "Speaking about what I do seems most unnatural to me," says Rosenthal. "It always has." His style has become well known gradually, through word-of-mouth about his boutique, sightings of the dazzling pieces worn by high-society clients, and the rare jewel that appears for sale in an auction catalogue. These glimpses have inspired countless followers and made the JAR mode the most influential look in *haute joaillerie* in the last decade of the twentieth century.

Joel Arthur Rosenthal in front of his Place Vendôme boutique in Paris.

JAR

When Joel Arthur Rosenthal opened his boutique JAR'S in Paris in 1977, he chose a location, 7 Place Vendôme, loaded with jewelry history. Fine French jewelers Van Cleef & Arpels, Boucheron, and Chaumet, among others, had made Place Vendôme the most prestigious address for jewelry in the world during the first half of the twentieth century when they created extravagant and imaginative work for royalty, movie stars, and style icons. Cartier did the same thing right around the corner on rue de la Paix. Keenly aware of the area's significance, Rosenthal set high standards for himself from the moment he started making precious accessories. It was an ambitious move considering he had very little experience in the field.

A native New Yorker, Rosenthal experimented in various creative endeavors before becoming a jewelry designer. After studying art history and philosophy at Harvard, he joined the film industry as a script writer for Otto Preminger's 1967 film *Hurry Sundown*. A few years later, when he could not raise the financing for his own screenplay, he turned his attention to design. Rosenthal, who had painted since he was a child, worked for Christian Dior and Nina Ricci in Paris, then opened

A pavé-set Montana sapphire and silver butterfly brooch made by JAR around 1987 has white diamonds in platinum on the wings, and rose diamonds in silver on the body. A 3.89-carat antique cushion-cut diamond shines at the center of the insect.

Greenhouse with Pierre Jeannet, a former psychiatrist. The chic little shop on the Left Bank sold embroidery canvases hand painted by Rosenthal. In the mid-seventies, he switched gears and went back to New York City to design jewelry for Bulgari while the Italian firm was at its creative peak. After six months, Rosenthal was transferred to Bulgari headquarters in Rome, but he did not go. Instead he decided to open his own jewelry boutique at Place Vendôme in Paris with Jeannet.

Rosenthal's jewelry attracted attention immediately because it was so different from anything being made at the time. Unorthodox materials such as ebony and real seashells from the seashore were one thing people noticed. Another thing was Rosenthal's clever reinterpretation of styles from the past, like his slender Art Deco style earrings. He transformed the jazz age accessory into a JAR original with elongated briolettes in pretty pastel gems, such as amethysts and pink topaz. But what really made Rosenthal stand out as a design innovator was his special pavé of precious and semiprecious stones.

Every detail—and there are many—in Rosenthal's precious pavé shows his artistic approach. First there are the gems. Rosenthal went beyond the fine jeweler's traditional palette of rubies, emeralds, blue sapphires, and white diamonds to stones like pink and violet sapphires, light green, brown, and rose-colored diamonds, and semiprecious stones such as amethysts, citrines, and garnets. He mixes modern and antique gem cuts to form areas of bright light and sections with less brilliance. To create gradations of color and add highlights and shadows, he uses different shades of one gem, as well as perfectly matched sets of gems.

His way with gems is beautifully demonstrated in his Butterfly Brooch made around 1987. The creature has a selection of light to dark blue-purple Montana sapphires on its wings, which are sliced with perfectly matched white diamond veins. Rose-colored diamonds, surrounding a 3.89-carat antique cushion-cut diamond, cover the body of the bug.

The metal mounting is the second part of the pavé. Rosenthal approaches metals in the same way he does gems— for their artistic possibilities. In the Butterfly Brooch he used platinum sparingly to brighten the diamonds on the veins of the wings. Oxidized silver is the mounting for the rest of the gems.

The moody black metal, a standard in Rosenthal's designs, was totally unorthodox when he introduced it in the 1980s. Fine jewelers had dropped silver from their repertoire about a hundred years earlier when they learned how to work platinum,

which heightens a gem's brilliance. Rosenthal, however, was not seeking that traditional effect. He used blackened silver for its dramatic appearance. The metal was a strong contrast to white diamonds and it outlined the various colors of other gems. Another thing oxidized silver did for JAR jewelry was add texture. The dark circles surrounding the stones made them look like stitches, giving Rosenthal's pavé a nubby appearance that harks back to his roots in embroidery.

In the Mogol Flower bracelet, made around 1987, Rosenthal used his pavé to capture the spirit of historical Indian art and textiles. To recreate the lack of perspective, or flat appearance of the buds and blooms in Indian work, Rosenthal set evenly matched selections of rubies, diamonds, sapphires, and amethysts in silver. He employed two types of green gems, tsavorites and tourmalines, mounted in gold to give a rippling effect to the curves of the stems. The background of the wide bracelet is made of oxidized titanium, an iridescent and atmospheric metal that changes appearance whenever it is moved. Its many colors make the solid surface of the bracelet seem like a luminous pool of swirling vapors.

From the moment Rosenthal found real estate and opened JAR'S at the most prestigious location for a jewelry store in the world, he managed to do just what he had intended—he followed the tradition of the Place Vendôme jewelers who worked in the glory design days before World War II. Like his predecessors, he has made original jewelry and attracted the bold name society set. Olimpia de Rothschild, Mica Ertegun, Jayne Wrightsman, Nan Kempner, Betsy Bloomingdale, and Susan Gutfreund are among his clients. These women appreciate his artistry. They also like the fact that he mainly makes one-of-a-kind jewels and will do commissions created specially for a client, like with haute couture. "He is a genius," Susan Gutfreund told *Vogue* in 1992. "And if you can live long enough, you have these things. Not everyone understands that he takes an engagement ring and you wait three years. But every single thing he has made for me I wear—and that's what jewelry should be about."

ESTABLISHED: 1973
FOUNDERS: Joel Rosenthal (born 1943) and Pierre Jeannet
EXHIBITION: 1987, New York. *A Collection of Jewels Created in Celebration of Our Ten Years in Place Vendôme*, The National Academy of Design.
LOCATION: Paris

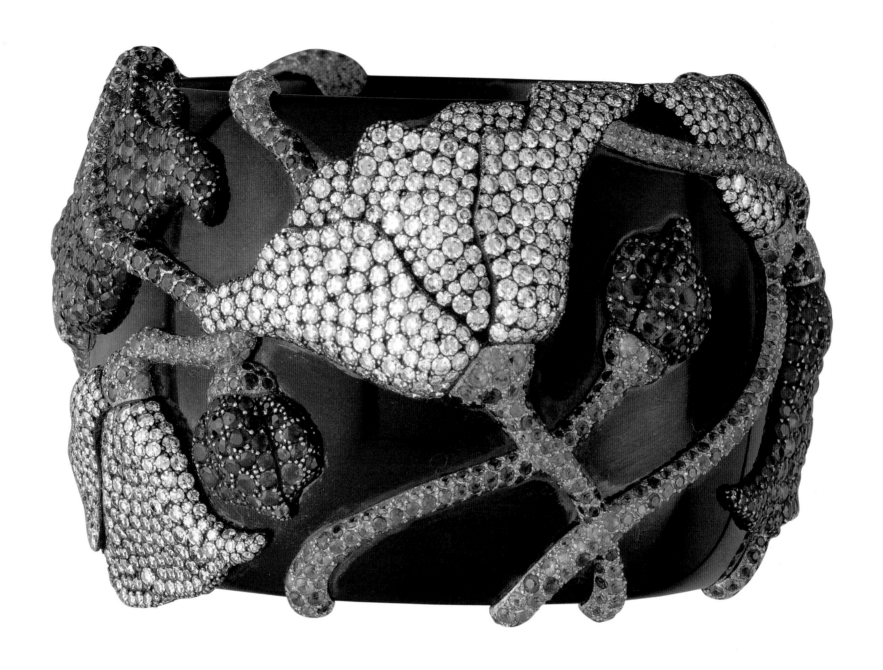

JAR's Mogol Flower bracelet, made around 1987, has
ruby, sapphire, diamond, amethyst, and silver flowers
on tzavorite, tourmaline, and gold stems, twining
around an oxidized titanium bangle.

EPILOGUE

At the end of the twentieth century, modern living became very high tech. Cell phones, e-mail, the internet, and gadgets like Palm Pilots changed the way people communicated, did business, and lived their lives. These technological advances made a science-fiction vision of the future seem like a reality. And they make it difficult to fathom what will occur in culture and society over the next hundred years.

In terms of jewelry, it seems probable, however, that the legacy of twentieth-century designers will endure. There were many styles and concepts developed that perfectly expressed contemporary culture, while also forming new genres. Many designers are already following in the footsteps of Hollywood insiders, signature stylists, rock hounds, and some of the other twentieth-century pioneers covered in this book. They approach jewelry the same way as their predecessors. Modern-day minimalists, for example, think like the vanguard of the seventies, that jewelry should be spare, follow the body's curves, and be easy to wear. Others who are currently working assume the maverick's audacious stance that gems should be used artistically to create a strong jewelry statement. What the newcomers add, how they develop the vocabulary of a genre, and the spin they put on the style are the details that make their work relevant.

The mix of cultural changes and design talent made the twentieth century an extraordinary era for jewelry. Designers were constantly asking themselves what it meant to be modern. And in the process they not only made original jewelry, they also came up with guidelines about what modern jewelry should be. Suzanne Belperron said jewelry should reflect a woman's personality. Salvador Dalí believed that jewelry should "uplift the spirit, stir the imagination, and express convictions." Jean Fouquet wrote prolifically about his view that jewelry should be bold, functional, and artistic. Above and beyond the designs, these words of wisdom and encouragement from twentieth-century master jewelers make them a resource that should inspire all kinds of creativity in the future.

Gwyneth Paltrow went down the red carpet at the 2000 Oscars in a Calvin Klein dress and a ruby and diamond tassel necklace and bracelet by Cathy Waterman. A Hollywood insider, Waterman, who is based in Los Angeles and counts many A-list stars among her clients, gets inspiration from several past periods, especially the Art Nouveau and Deco eras.

Courtney Love stood out in a white Versace dress and a minimal diamond lariat necklace by Stefan Hafner at the 1997 Oscars. Hafner, an Italian jewelry designer who has added a lot of high glamour to modern minimalism with his diamond necklaces, gets a sultry effect by using just a handful of stones—and by designing, he says, "with air, leaving a lot of empty space."

The imaginative H$_2$O necklace from Chanel's 1999 Passages collection has a precious pavé of dark blue sapphires grading into light blue sapphires, and then diamonds. The changing colors of the gems give the water drops the illusion of movement.

MANY THANKS

First and foremost we thank Ralph Esmerian, to whom this book is dedicated. His knowledge and passion for jewelry is our inspiration. We also must give credit where credit is due to Bob Morton, who has given the green light to all our projects with Abrams and taught us so much about making books.

We are very grateful to the following designers, jewelers, jewelry historians, auctioneers, and publicists. Without these people Bejeweled would still be just an idea: Frank Acaro, Ilaria Alber, Sigrid Barten, Carol Brodie Gelles, Linda Buckley, Nicolas Bulgari, Simon Critchell, Robin Davis, Yamile Diaz, Pam Eldridge, Anne Fahey, Krista Florin, Audrey Friedman, Robert M. Gibson, Fernanda Gilligan, Christine Goppel, Bernard and Peggy Grosz, Jim Haag, Stephan Hafner, Pierre Jeannet, Kathy Kermian, Barry Kieselstein-Cord, Edward Landrigan, Fred Leighton, Mara Leighton, Robert Lee Morris, Daphne Lingon, Pierce MacGuire, Eric Nussbaum, Elsa Peretti, Paloma Picasso, Muffie Potter, Joel Arthur Rosenthal, Bonnie Selfe, Rebecca Selva, Tracy Strong, Simon Teakle, John Ullmann, Valerie Vlasaty, Cathy Waterman, Ronald Winston, David and Sybil Yurman, and Janet Zapata. While we were writing this book, Paul Flato, an American jewelry legend, passed away. He was an absolute original and it was an honor to know him and his daughter Catherine Dennis.

We are deeply appreciative for the day-to-day support of Trudy Tripolone, Saralee Smithwick, and Janet Bliss, and the unique assistance of Cher, Loree Rodkin, Donna Karan, and our agent Nancy Trichter. To all of our friends and family who stood by us in the years it took to write this book—you know who you are—we love you and thank you.

Since 1996 when we began contributing to In Style, there have been almost as many editors in our lives as jewelry designers. We are grateful to so many who have been influential and supportive of our work, especially Martha Nelson, Charla Lawhon, Hal Rubenstein, Cindy Weber Cleary, Lisa Arbetter, and Jackie Goewey. We also send thanks to Patrice Adcroft of Seventeen and the multitalented Lisa Gabor.

Photographs are a huge part of Bejeweled. Thanks to the many photographers and archivists who provided us with images, particularly David Behl, who photographed most of the jewelry in the book, and Justin White, who provided an amazing moment.

The Bejeweled dream team bedazzled us with their brilliance. A super-size thanks to In Style Art Director Garrett Yankou (rhymes with thank you) for the stunning cover design and moonlighting time. Gigantic thanks to Carol Robson, whose deft design touch makes the book flow from the first page to the last. And last but far from least, we are deeply indebted to our editor, Ellen Nidy, who gave us our title and much more. We thank Ellen for her enthusiasm, ideas, and most of all, sharing our vision of a little book on a big topic.

PENNY PRODDOW
MARION FASEL
NEW YORK CITY, 2001

Index

Page numbers in italics refer to picture captions.

Photo credits

Photo research by Photosearch, Inc. Endpapers: courtesy of Tiffany; 2: © David Behl; 3: © David Behl; 5: courtesy of Verdura; 6: courtesy of Sotheby's; 7: © 2001 Estate of Alexander Calder/Artist Rights Society (ARS), New York. © David Behl; 8: © David Behl; 10, left: © 2001 Artists Rights Society (ARS), New York/ADAGP, Paris. © David Behl; 10, right: © 2001 Artists Rights Society (ARS), New York/ADAGP, Paris. © David Behl; 11: © David Behl; 13: © David Behl; 14: © Collection VIOLLET; 15: The Kobal Collection; 16: Frank Edwards/Fotos International/Archive Photos; 17: Brown Brothers; 18: © David Behl; 19: © David Behl; 20, left: © David Behl; 20, right: courtesy of Tiffany; 22, right: Museum of Modern Art/Film Stills Archive; 22, left: courtesy of Christie's; 23, left: courtesy of Sotheby's; 23, right: Press Association Photos Limited; 24, left: © Cecil Beaton Photograph, courtesy of Sotheby's London; 24, right: Nick Welsh © Collection "Art de Cartier"; 25: © Cecil Beaton Photograph, courtesy of Sotheby's London; 26: courtesy of private collection, New York; 27: © David Behl; 28: photograph of Barbara Hutton, courtesy of Sotheby's, London; brooches, © David Behl; 29, left: drawing and brooch © David Behl; 29, right: Edward Carswell, © *Vogue*, Condé Nast Publications, Inc. (*Vogue* 12/1/1941 p. 87); 30: © David Behl; 31, right top: Eliot Elisofon/TimePix/LIFE Magazine © Time Inc.; 31, bottom: courtesy of Christie's; 32: courtesy of Bulgari; 33, lower left: courtesy of Bulgari; 33, upper right: courtesy of Christie's; 34: © 1972 Richard Avedon. Courtesy of *Vogue*, Condé Nast Publications, Inc.; 35: © 1972 Richard Avedon. Courtesy of *Vogue*, Condé Nast Publications, Inc.; 36: © David Behl; 37: courtesy of Bulgari; 38: courtesy of Sigrid Barten; 39: © 2001 Artists Rights Society (ARS), New York/ADAGP, Paris. © David Behl; 40, left: © David Behl; 40, right: Lafayette Studio, Paris. Private Collection. Courtesy Musée des Arts Décoratifs, Paris. All rights reserved; 41: © David Behl; 42, left: © 2001 Artists Rights Society (ARS), New York/ADAGP, Paris. © David Behl; 42, right: Vever Photography Archives. Courtesy Musée des Arts Décoratifs, Paris. All rights reserved; 43, left: © David Behl; 43, right: © David Behl; 44: courtesy of the Silver Collection; 45, top: Musée des Arts Décoratifs, Paris. All rights reserved; 45, bottom: © Photothèque des Musées de la Ville de Paris; 46, left: Fouquet Photography Archives. Courtesy Musée des Arts Décoratifs, Paris. All rights reserved; 46, right: courtesy

of private collection, New York; 47: © David Behl; 48: © David Behl; 49, right: Henri Vever Papers, Freer Gallery of Art and Arthur M. Sackler Gallery Archives, Smithsonian Institution, Washington D.C.; 51, left: © David Behl; 51, right: © David Behl; 52: Courtesy of Plattsburgh State Art Museum, Rockwell Kent Gallery and Collection; 53, left: © David Behl; 53, right: © David Behl; 54: © David Behl; 55: All rights reserved, The Metropolitan Museum of Art; 56: The Metropolitan Museum of Art. Promised gift of Linden Havemeyer Wise. (L.1996.69); 57, top, middle, and bottom: © David Behl; 59: photo by d'Ora; 60, top: Charlotte Perriand Archives/©2001 Artists Rights Society (ARS), New York/ADAGP, Paris; 60, bottom: © 2001 Man Ray Trust/Artists Rights Society (ARS), New York/ADAGP, Paris/Telimage; 61: © David Behl; 62: © David Behl; 63: © David Behl; 65: © David Behl; 67: © David Behl; 68, top: © David Behl; 68, bottom: © David Behl; 69: © David Behl; 70: © David Behl; 71: © David Behl; 72: courtesy of Paul Flato; 73, left bottom: Museum of Modern Art/Film Stills Archive; 73, right top: Museum of Modern Art/Film Stills Archive; 73, right bottom: Museum of Modern Art/Film Stills Archive; 73, left top: Bettmann/Corbis; 74, left: courtesy of Paul Flato; 74, right: © David Behl; 75: © David Behl; 77: Bettmann /Corbis; 78: The Kobal Collection; 79: courtesy of Sotheby's; 80: © 2001 Pedro E. Guerrero; 81: Philippe Halsman © Halsman Estate; 82, top: © Archivo Cameraphoto Epoche, Venice; 82: © 2001 Estate of Alexander Calder/Artist Rights Society (ARS), New York. © David Behl; 83: © 2001 Estate of Alexander Calder /Artist Rights Society (ARS), New York; 84: Agnes Varda/Agence Enguerand, Paris; 85: © 2001 Estate of Alexander Calder /Artist Rights Society (ARS), New York. © David Behl; 86: courtesy of Christie's; 87: © 2001 Kingdom of Spain Gala – Salvador Dali FoundationArtists Rights Society (ARS), New York. © David Behl; 88, top: © 2001 Kingdom of Spain Gala – Salvador Dali Foundation/Artists Rights Society (ARS), New York/Christie's Images, New York; 88, bottom right: © 2001 Kingdom of Spain Gala – Salvador Dali Foundation/Artists Rights Society (ARS), New York/Christie's Images, New York; 88, bottom left: courtesy of Christie's; 90: © David Behl; 91, left: John Rawlings, ©*Vogue*, Condé Nast Publications, Inc.; 91, right: courtesy of Sotheby's; 92: © Cecil Beaton Photograph, courtesy of Sotheby's London; 93: courtesy of Sotheby's; 94: courtesy of